ADVANCE PRAISE FOR THE POWER PATH

"...a unique and extraordinary gift to Western culture."
— John P. Milton, author and founder
of Sacred Passage and the Way of Nature Foundation

"A superb book, crammed full of practical advice."
— W. Brian Arthur, economist and business thought leader

"Get ready to be delightfully surprised. This book will expand your horizons and inspire you each step of the way."
— Sobonfu Somé, author of *Welcoming Spirit Home*

"Today's world urgently needs to bring the medicine of the Spirit into the business world. *The Power Path* contributes to this task by connecting what has been seen as two opposites: shamanism — which is devoted to service — and business — which is mistakenly thought of as just devoted to personal gain."
— Victor Sanchez, author of
The Teachings of Don Carlos and *Toltecs of the New Millenium*

"*The Power Path* is an excellent guide to living a better life. José and Lena have spent years studying knowledge, power, and spirituality and this book is an important means of sharing what has been learned. A gift from the heart...."
— Mark Meuller, trial lawyer and
representative for Native American tribal concerns

"*The Power Path* will help anyone interested in becoming a better manager or leader to understand and communicate with different types of people more effectively, develop greater awareness of opportunities, work cooperatively in teams, accept challenges, understand what is possible and realistic, and understand the behavior of adversaries — in short, to build cooperation and effectiveness, lessen conflicts, and achieve better results."
— Guy Saperstein, civil rights attorney and
trustee of the Sierra Club Foundation

"If you examine the failure of many companies to perform to their fullest potential, you will find that they haven't paid attention to the principles in this book. Drawing on lessons that have proven themselves over thousands of years, Stevens makes the power of ancient wisdom available for use in a modern business context. It's all about becoming more powerful, not in the sense of using force, but in the sense of bringing genuine vitality and effectiveness where it counts."
— Charles E. Smith, Ph.D., international organization development consultant and author of *The Merlin Factor*

"The Power Path sheds a bright clear light on the nature of power. José outlines the techniques and strategies that allow us to gather power and utilize it in an effective and responsible manner."
— Laurie Skreslet, mountain guide, inspirational speaker, and first Canadian to summit Mt. Everest

"Philanthropists are people of power, and philanthropy means the love of humankind. Those who give and those who receive will enjoy this book for it reveals the true nature and place of power and how it can be used with integrity and honesty."
— Jerry Mapp, president and CEO of California Pacific Medical Foundation

"The concepts in *The Power Path* may seem a little simple; but, then again, they may just be simply true. Having just read the book, I'm already referring back to it for reinforcement. I believe that José Stevens is on the right path."
— Michael Ochs, CEO, The Michael Ochs Archives. Com, the photographic archive of musicians

"Many of the most important lessons I've learned in life have been taught to me by José and Lena Stevens."
— Scott Carter, former executive producer for *Politcally Incorrect with Bill Maher* and currently producing *The Conspiracy Zone with Kevin Nealon*

"Incorporating discipline, spirituality, and inner perspective is vital in our work field. This book lets you open your eyes wider to see people and events at a much deeper level."
— Kidada Jones, designer

THE
POWER PATH

Also by José Stevens

Secrets of Shamanism:
Tapping the Spiritual Power within You

Transforming Your Dragons:
Turning Fear Patterns into Personal Power

THE
POWER PATH

The Shaman's Way to Success
in Business and Life

JOSÉ STEVENS, Ph.D.
with LENA STEVENS

NEW WORLD LIBRARY
NOVATO, CALIFORNIA

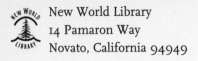 New World Library
14 Pamaron Way
Novato, California 94949

Library of Congress Cataloging-in-Publication Data
Stevens, José.
  The power path : the shaman's way to success in business
and life / José Stevens, with Lena Stevens.
     p.   cm.
Includes index.
  ISBN 1-57731-217-1 (pbk. : alk. paper)
1. Interpersonal communication. 2. Shamanism. 3. Personnel
management. I. Title: Shaman's way to success in business
and life. II. Stevens, Lena. III. Title.
HM1166 .S74 2002
302.2—dc21   2002001122

First Printing, May 2002
ISBN 1-57731-217-1
Printed in Canada on acid-free, partially recycled paper
Distributed to the trade by Publishers Group West

10 9 8 7 6 5 4 3 2 1

This book is dedicated with respect and honor to our
friend and teacher Gaudalupe Candelario Avila,
Huichol maracame shaman,
a true man of knowledge and light.
May his courage and bright spirit continue
to influence and spread wisdom wherever it is needed.
And to the men and women of knowledge everywhere,
may your power and vision midwife us
into a brighter world.

CONTENTS

Acknowledgments

To all our clients and colleagues in the business world
who have taught us so much.
To our indigenous teachers and friends.
To our students and fellow searchers
who have encouraged us beyond measure.
To our wonderful agent, Wendy Keller.
To our publisher, New World Library,
who had the courage to publish a book bridging fields.
To our family who sacrificed so that this book
could be written.

We thank you deeply.

Introduction

Leadership is about creating a domain in which human beings continually deepen their understanding of reality and become more capable of participating in the unfolding of the world. Ultimately, leadership is about creating new realities.... The new leadership must be grounded in fundamentally new understandings of how the world works.

— Peter Senge, *Synchronicity: The Inner Path of Leadership*

The World that we perceive, such as the self (our own ego), is nothing more than a description—a fantasy that only seems real due to our insistence in acting as though it were real.... If we stop our contradictory description of the world, which we construct daily, we see that it is the true path to freedom that allows us to construct better worlds for us to inhabit.

— Victor Sanchez, *Toltecs of the New Millennium*

- Corporate leader
- Chief executive officer
- Chief financial officer
- Chief information officer
- President
- Vice president
- Head of human resources
- Manager
- Trainer
- Team leader
- Director
- Communication officer
- Employer
- Owner
- Supervisor
- Board member
- Department head
- Businessperson

Those are the highly recognizable titles of modern business leaders, the movers and shakers of corporations that shape today's world and dictate the course of so much of the world's progress.

- Wise man
- Medicine woman
- *Curandero*
- Healer
- Shaman
- *Maracame*
- Wizard
- Spirit walker
- Soul retriever
- Visionary
- Medium
- Storyteller
- Seer
- Prophet
- Teacher
- Sorcerer
- Psychopomp (Walker between the Worlds)

These are just a few names applied to extraordinary men and women who have acted as leaders of their indigenous communities on every continent of this planet. They have been the movers and shakers of their worlds, the ones who have made things happen despite massive obstacles and unfavorable odds.

What, if anything, do these two apparently diverse groups have in common? Is there a relationship between them? Is there anything to be learned from the mystically oriented indigenous leaders that can apply to the modern business community? At first glance it may be difficult to see the connection between these worlds; with closer scrutiny, however, you will find within the indigenous traditions a vast and deep knowledge base crucial to the businessperson who is ready to understand the next phase and take the next leap in the business world.

When you stop to consider, is there such a difference between the challenges of a medicine man or woman confronted with a patient's illness and a business consultant confronted with a seriously fractured corporation? When a seer is asked to predict the outcome of the hunt, is that such a different circumstance from a marketing expert attempting to predict the outcome of an advertising campaign? When a shaman is asked to remove a curse, is that not like a manager being asked to find out about and remove the obstacles to productivity within a department? The obstacles and challenges are actually not so different. The difference lies in how each group traditionally sees the problem and how they go about attempting to fix it.

For years our business has been to live in both of these worlds, studying with mystics privately and outwardly working as executive coaches and trainers. The theme of power is central to both worlds, and we discovered that we could be more influential individually and as consultants if we trained in the ancient methods of acquiring and utilizing power.

The knowledge gained from our apprenticeships is the very thing that has helped us be effective with our business clients. We have learned much about the nature and structure of communities and groups of people who employ tried and true methods and models for effective communication, problem solving, survival, and power. When translated to the modern-day group or community of the business organization, these models provide a new means to attain the successful results that everyone is looking for.

In the late 1980s, through a close friend, we met an indigenous healer visiting from Mexico, a man who immeasurably impressed us and was to indelibly change the course of our lives. As we got to know him, we realized we had met a rare man of great integrity, a man who could teach us the shamanic way based on ancient tradition.

We began an apprenticeship with him — with trepidation and excitement — that was to last ten years until his death in 1999. He was from the Huichol tradition, a *maracame,* an important shaman to his people in the rugged Sierra Madre of central Mexico. With this powerful yet gentle man we had some of the most harrowing and enlightening experiences of our lives. During this time, with our teacher's encouragement, we traveled many times deep into the harsh deserts of central Mexico and to the jungles of the Amazon in Peru to study with shamans there. These intensely difficult and rewarding experiences gave us many insights into the true structure of power.

All the while we maintained and developed our work lives as seminar leaders, lecturers, coaches, and trainers, rarely mentioning a word about our journeys to Peru and Mexico except to our most trusted friends. The effect of our experiences, however, directly translated to our work with a great variety of clients, both individual and corporate. We assisted lawyers in winning their cases and CEOs in solving management problems, and we helped countless working people discover their path of power.

In this book we share the knowledge and basic structures that form the foundation of our work with people in helping them to find their path of power. Rather than long excursions into theories and philosophies, you will find here a synthesis of the core of what we have learned about the power path from our much loved indigenous teachers, the unobtrusive shamans we have spent time with, and from our own experiences in business.

For simplicity we are going to use the term *shaman* to represent a variety of indigenous leaders. Technically there are many differences between sorcerers, *curanderos*, mediums, and medicine men and women. This is not the place, however, to consider those differences; our goal here is to expose their nearly universal understandings about the nature of power.

What Is a Shaman?

Shaman is an ancient Siberian word meaning "to see." A shaman is also a community leader, an exceptional individual who stands out for his or her superior talent as a prophet, healer, warrior-protector, storyteller par excellence, and/or man or woman of knowledge. Shamans' communities recognize them as the ones to go to in times of difficulty, the carriers of the solution, the ones with answers to questions and with the clarity to envision the probable outcomes of particular actions.

Often they are the chiefs of their tribe and make major decisions that affect the survival of everyone. Shamans in all parts of the world exhibit remarkably similar and consistent philosophies and practices. Every major culture has a shamanic tradition, perhaps often hidden to us, but whose occasional surface ripples hint at the massive undercurrent that courses below.

We name our vehicles and sports teams after animals, never realizing that this is an ancient shamanic practice meant to draw power from nature, the world of the animal spirits. Natural medicine is another shamanic practice we've inherited. We advertise and promote the benefits of herbs and plants that heal without the harmful side effects of laboratory chemicals.

Yet in the process of proclaiming ourselves an advanced, scientifically minded people, we have forgotten our roots, the reality that reminds us of an essential, hidden knowledge — the wisdom of the shamans.

One of the core activities of shamans around the world is accumulating power, the power to carry out their duties as healers, prophets, and guides for their peoples. Without sufficient power, shamans are vulnerable to the elements of nature and helpless in the face of disease, dysfunction, and spiritual malaise. A shaman without power can accomplish nothing. To understand a shaman's perspective is to understand how they view power and how they go about accumulating it.

In *The Power Path* we focus specifically on how shamans understand the world in terms of their power, because for a shaman power is the name of the game. Our focus is on the nature of power and the rules of power according to shamanic tradition. You will see that this knowledge is as applicable today as it has always been. This secret knowledge is as valuable in today's business jungle as it is in the Amazon jungles or anywhere else indigenous people struggle for survival.

SUMMARY

Important Concepts to Remember

- Shamans and business leaders have much in common. Both are

    1. Problem solvers.
    2. Leaders to their people.
    3. Viewers of the big picture.
    4. Forecasters of events.

- Shamans accumulate power just as business leaders do, but from a different context.
- Shamanic rules about power can help us in business and in our lives. To learn these rules, read on.

Part 1

DEFINING POWER

Chapter 1

WHAT POWER IS

Probably the central concept of shamanism, wherever in this world it is found, is the idea of power. Simply stated, this is the notion that underlying all the visible forms in the world, animate and inanimate, there exists a vital essence from which these forms emerge and by which they are nurtured. Ultimately everything returns to this ineffable, mysterious, impersonal unknown.

— Douglas Sharon, *Wizard of the Four Winds: A Shaman's Story*

Whether you like it or not, the game of life here on the planet is all about power: striving for it, achieving it, holding on to it, manipulating it, giving it away, giving it up, losing it, stealing it, fearing it, lusting for it, trading it, investing in it, searching for it, learning about it, and mastering it. If you say you are not interested in power, that you are above or beyond it, that you think it is overrated, that you believe it is the

root of all evils, or that the world would be a better place
without such emphasis on it, then you are fooling yourself dramatically.

On the other hand, if your life is consumed with
lust for power, drawn by its magnetism to accumulate
and manipulate it, then paradoxically, chances are that
this ambition actually stems from a foundation of feeling rather powerless. Either way — if you devalue its
importance or make it into some kind of god — you are
failing to appreciate and understand the true nature of
power. It is critical that you learn its secrets if you hope
to ever wield it effectively.

The great irony is that, although life is a game of
power, few people actually know very much about its
underlying nature. Certainly most people do not know
the rules of power because, if they did, they would
manifest their knowledge of power and be completely
comfortable with all facets of it. There would be less
obsession and dysfunctional ambition on the one hand
and less sense of feeling powerless in life on the other.

If power is so fundamental to life, then how has
this lack of knowledge come to be? We can simply say
that part of what makes the game of life so interesting
is that such things as the rules of power tend to remain
hidden right under our noses. Long ago shamans fig-
ured out that the game is to discover these rules and
put the knowledge to use for the benefit of themselves
and others. This knowledge is available to each of
us, and it can bring us success in business and in all
areas of our lives.

Without this shamanic insight into the nature of reality, we often don't even realize that anything is hidden, and we mistake the superficial for reality. We don't see reality, and so we accept pale and weak substitutes for it instead. These substitutes are like beautiful flowers made from plastic, silk, or paper: colorful but without life and scent. The business world has many examples of this. An organization may have the most beautiful offices with all the latest expensive furniture, computers, and technology, but if communication problems, depression, and a lack of enthusiasm and direction exist among the staff, then this organization is not a success. An inattentive outsider may notice only a glittering but false power without seeing any of the powerlessness and weakness beneath.

The game that shamans discovered is first to realize that the real goods are hidden right in front of us and then to go about finding them. You will find the hidden power in the real resources of a troubled company — its people, their potential, and their philosophies and attitudes.

AN EXAMINATION
OF POWER

What is this power that is necessary to win in the game of life and in the game of business? What is the power that allows you to walk the power path? We need to first come up with a working definition of power. The dictionary states that the word *power* comes from the Latin *potere,* meaning "to be able." That is a good start in our definition: To succeed in anything in life, you must first be able. That is why power is the key ingredient in the grand game. To be able implies that we are able to learn something, that we are capable; it does not necessarily imply that we already know how to do something, so it refers to potential, to capacity.

Power then is potential.

That fits our shamanic understanding of power. Successful businesses will often attribute their performance to the fact that they recognized the potential in something — a product, an employee, a direction, or an opportunity. You could say that recognizing the power in something is then *recognizing its potential* — its ability, or its gifts.

The dictionary also refers to power as "strength, might, force, control, ascendancy, legal ability, influence, force, and momentum." This sounds like a good definition, but it can be very misleading, implying that strength, force, or control will make a business successful. However, we have seen over and over that this is not necessarily the case. Vietnam, for example, was a wake-up call, teaching Americans that winning a war takes more than overwhelming military strength. Another common perception is that if you just exert more force you will be more successful; however, once again this strategy has proven to fail. Business language is filled with adages inviting us to use brute force to achieve our objectives: "Destroy the competition,"

"Divide and conquer," "Beat the odds," and "Battle to the top" are but a few examples.

Many martial arts demonstrate that the more force and momentum used by an attacker, the greater the attacker's fall and defeat. Reflect on your own observations. You can see that more willpower, enthusiasm, and hard work do not necessarily translate to being more powerful. Obviously none of these things guarantees winning. Perhaps the emphasis on brute force has been a disservice and we have failed, and continue to fail, to notice something more important about power that is hidden right in front of us.

We all become culturally imprinted about what power is supposed to look like in the context of the times and society we live in. Its visible forms are clear to everyone living in a particular society. In modern times the symbols of power include everything from badges, diplomas, and testimonials to expensive suits, limousines, and private jets. We see these marks of power and automatically think in terms of hierarchy, top to bottom, winners and losers, and we assume the bearers of these symbols are highly successful.

Bear in mind, however, that in today's world most of these badges of power can be purchased for a price. Most forms of modern power are tied to money, and money is seen as powerful. No one can argue that point, nor are we objecting to it.

Certainly money is a most powerful external ingredient in getting things done in the business world, and yet we have seen corporations with almost unlimited resources founder because of poor decision making, and we have seen backyard garage-based businesses that function on a shoestring grow into megacorporations. So obviously money is not a guarantee of power in the modern world. How money is used is what counts, and its skillful use is based on a power that is not so obvious.

Power in a shamanic sense and from our experience is not primarily about force, physical strength, momentum, control, might, or money. The primary term shamans include in their definition of power is the word *energy* — the capacity for vigorous activity, the ability to act with potency. So power to a shaman means available energy, vigor, capacity, and the potential to serve, influence, and make a difference according to will and intent; it also means to enter into deeper levels of awareness to access knowledge, peer into the future, perceive secrets, remove obstacles, and enter the dynamic flow where effort ceases and nature takes over. Perhaps, this kind of power is valuable for business and organizational leaders as well.

Shamans spend their entire lives learning, discovering, and walking the path of power, exercising and developing their ability to manifest power in a way that brings the best results and the minimum of negative consequences. They are thus the world's foremost experts in the ways of power and in walking the challenging and fascinating trail that leads them to become what they call a man or woman of knowledge. This trail leads them to discover that the greatest of powers are those that are not on everyday display, not manifested outwardly for all the world to see, and definitely not advertised.

To understand the power that is not so obvious, let us first take a look at the fundamental rules of power according to shamanic understanding. These rules are implicit in the shamanic world, having been preserved in oral traditions and never recorded in an official shamanic text or manual. Certainly you can find allusions to them in the writings of various popular authors such as Deepak Chopra, Miguel Ruiz, and Carlos Castaneda. You will not, however, find the fundamentals of shamanic power laid out all in one place as they are here.

Yet, if you were to travel the world and question wise elders and shamans from Siberia, central Australia, the Amazon, the Himalayas, the plains of North America, the vast reaches of Africa, the tropical islands of the South Pacific, the humid climes of Southeast Asia, the far northern tundra, or anywhere for that matter, you will find for the most part an implicit agreement about these ten rules of power that you are about to learn in the next chapter. This is striking when you consider that these community leaders have had no contact with one another, no cell phones, no e-mail, no universities, no international networks of any visible kind. Their only point of contact is the dreamtime, the spirit world, the invisible reality — and they have never had to worry about a computer virus or sunspot activity shutting down that system. Our motivation in bringing this information to you by translating it into modern business terminology is to provide you the same wisdom, insights, and tools that have been available to these indigenous communities for centuries. When you apply these tools to business, you become better at the game, but it won't turn you into a shaman. That takes years of specific training within a unique tradition.

SUMMARY

Important Concepts to Remember

- Life on earth is all about power.
- The rules governing power remain somewhat hidden.
- Shamans know the rules and apply them with great success.
- The word *shaman* means to see or one who sees.
- To have power means to be able, to have potential, to have the vigor or energy to do.
- To have power then means to be able to see potential wherever it lies, within oneself, in a situation, or in other people.

Chapter 2

THE BASIC SHAMANIC RULES OF POWER

I know that every time in my life that I've run across simple
rules giving rise to emergent, complex messiness, I've just
said, "Ah, isn't that lovely!" And I think sometimes, when
other people run across them, they recoil.

— Brian Arthur, Citibank professor in economics, *Complexity:
The Emerging Science at the Edge of Order and Chaos*

Each system has its own rule, its own way of relating to the
cosmos. Each rule provides the logic — the building blocks
of knowledge — that maps out the specific tradition. . . . By
following a well-drawn map, you get where you want to
go . . . accordingly, the rule offers guidance for participating
with Spirit.

— Ken Eagle Feather, *A Toltec Path*

There is a set of core rules of power that has been
understood and practiced with discipline by
people using techniques of shamanism throughout
history and in all the cultures of the world. You will

find that some of the rules are very simple and some
are quite complex when you explore their implications.
Some of the rules contain a number of sub-rules. We
will discuss all the rules and their aspects at length
throughout the body of this book. These rules are listed
in no special order, and each stands on its own, complete unto itself.

RULE I

All objects in the universe are following the path of power.

A. Everything in the universe manifests the
   amount of power it has gained thus far.
B. More powerful objects make it possible for
   objects with less power to become more
   powerful.

If you consider the natural environment, you will
notice that this is true. For example, a tree can only
manifest the amount of power it has collected and
gained in its life with the help of more powerful objects
such as the sun, the nutritional system in the earth, and
the element of water.

If you consider human-made environments, you'll
see this rule still holds true. For example, at any given
moment a business will manifest only the amount
of power it has gained up to that time with the help of
larger systems of knowledge, information, support, and
resources.

RULE 2

Power stems from four primary sources:
(1) inspiration; (2) simplicity;
(3) exchange; and (4) conception.

A business's path of power stems from the same four sources. The inspiration, spirit, and enthusiasm generated around the conception and birth of a project, business, or idea can play a big role in its ultimate success. Likewise, simplicity and singularity of focus are exceptionally important for the success of any business. To maintain its path of power, a business must create clear avenues of exchange between its departments and with systems that lie outside the organization.

RULE 3

Power in itself is neutral.
It is neither good nor bad.
It just is. How you manage it
determines the positive or negative consequences
for you and others.

The management of power is similar to the management of time. In a business environment with deadlines and multiple tasks, you must identify what undermines and depletes your power as well as what management practices and attitudes increase your abilities and performance.

RULE 4

The path of power is expensive: There is always a price to pay for real power.

You may bid for power at any time, but you will be tested to see if you are ready and deserving. Being on the path of power includes being on the path of truth, love, integrity, and service. The price of power is related in part to giving up the limitations of the personality, habits of fear, inadequacy, blame, and judgment. Bidding for power when you are not ready is extremely costly; not bidding for power when you are ready is a lost opportunity.

RULE 5

Power can be manifested only when you focus your attention and intention in the present.

This truth is critical to stalking power. Power is a product of intention. It is only available to you in full when you put your attention in the here and now. You will notice that you can only influence an outcome by what you do in the present. Therefore, if you focus your full attention in the present, much more power will go into your intention.

What keeps an individual or business from being able to focus 100 percent in the present is the non-acceptance of or resistance to the present by having, for example, unrealistic expectations or worry over past failures. A most valuable lesson we learned from our indigenous friends was the need to be fully accepting of whatever *is*, without judgment. Only then can you focus fully on the present and from that point make changes through your intentions.

RULE 6

Power can be hunted and gained in ways similar to the rules of the hunt in the natural environment.

In order to walk the path of power in business, you must learn to stalk power — to observe it, understand it, know its habits, and then pounce on it with perfect timing. This requires preparation, patience, readiness, and the ability to act with lightning speed and precision at the most opportune moment. There can be no obsessing, second-guessing, worry, or expectations, or the hunt will be unsuccessful.

RULE 7

Power must be ridden as a surfer rides a wave: balance is everything on the power path.

The ability to manage, understand, and hold power is determined in part by how flexible an individual or business is willing and able to be. Ups and downs, productive and nonproductive times, expansion and contraction are just a few of the aspects that require balance to stay on the path of power and not be thrown off it.

RULE 8

*All power manifests through four aspects:
breath, light, sound, and intent;
these aspects form the basis of communication.*

Communication is a crucial component of any successful business or community. Communication is much more than just the words you speak; it has to do with your attitude, feelings, thoughts, actions, and ultimately the essence of who you are. A more powerful and shamanic basis of communication is necessary to fuel your intentions.

RULE 9

*All real power has light as its one true source;
the power path that manifests light
is the path of love, the path with heart.*

In a business environment this path of love or heart translates as the power of manifesting your true work and true essence, and the acknowledgment of your individuality, service, value, character, and spirit. Recognition, respect, and gratitude in the workplace are all in keeping with this rule.

RULE 10

*The smaller the degree of separation,
the greater the power available.*

This rule is related to understanding paradoxes. If you look at nature, you will see many individual forms: individual plants, rocks, trees, bodies of water, mountains, and valleys. Each form has its own character, spirit, personality, and potential relationship to you. The paradox is that each form is interconnected and an inseparable part of the whole, vast organism we call nature. Moreover, each form and system in nature is interdependent; what happens to one affects all others. This is true in all aspects of life and no less so in business. Certainly both individuality and speciality in individuals and businesses exist, and this uniqueness keeps life interesting; but there is also a need to see the connectedness to the whole, for the whole is the greater power source for the individual.

Perhaps as you read through these ten rules you will instantly sense the truth and meaning in them without knowing exactly how or why. If you do, it suggests that you have already been operating to a degree according to the more shamanic way of perceiving. After all, these truths are universal, and while they more obviously underlie the practices in indigenous, shamanically based cultures, they are certainly not confined to that world. The truth is the truth is the truth, no matter who perceives and acts upon it. Nevertheless, by reading further you can refine your understanding, increase your shamanic skills of perception, and learn to become more powerful.

If, on the other hand, these rules baffled you or you

cannot grasp what they might have to do with you as a businessperson, then this book can help you go further than you have gone before. Our purpose in writing this book is to open the doors of understanding for you and encourage you to walk through them on your path to achieving true power.

SUMMARY

Important Concepts to Remember

There are the ten shamanic rules of power:
- Rule 1. Everything follows the path of power.
- Rule 2. The path of power is sourced in four things: inspiration, simplicity, exchange, and conception.
- Rule 3. Power is neutral, not good or bad.
- Rule 4. There is always a price to more power.
- Rule 5. Power rests upon intention and attention in the present moment.
- Rule 6. Power can be stalked, hunted, and won.
- Rule 7. Power must be balanced.
- Rule 8. Power manifests through four aspects: breath, light, sound, and intent.
- Rule 9. The power path is the path with heart.
- Rule 10. The smaller the degree of separation, the greater the power available.

Chapter 3

HOW SHAMANS SEE
THE WORLD

Seeing is not difficult. What is difficult is breaking the retaining wall in our minds which holds our perception in place.

— Carlos Castaneda, *The Art of Dreaming*

There are those rare and precious moments when it seems as if a window opens onto our soul and we catch a glimpse into ways of knowing and communicating of which we had no previous knowledge.

— David Korten,
The Post-Corporate World: Life After Capitalism

THE GAME OF LIFE
AND BUSINESS

We have briefly seen how important power is to shamans the world over, explored how they understand the nature of power, and reviewed the ten shamanic rules of power. Let us now look at another important aspect of the game of life: how shamans see the world and how they approach life in a way that ensures them health, well-being, and excellent leadership skills.

To understand this aspect of power, we need to know how shamans cultivate power and how they use it for their specific intentions and purposes. We need to know how they develop balance and rhythm, form a firm grip on external reality, and gain a strong grasp of myth, metaphor, and the amazing worlds within. We need to know how they steer clear of neurosis and depression and yet tackle the great challenges of life while taking responsibility for the health and well-being of their fellows. Why is this knowledge helpful? Because for centuries these individuals have been highly successful at many of the very things that challenge modern businesspeople, such as problem solving, people management, handling competition, dealing with crises, and coping with change.

Simple Principles of the Game of Life

The following simple principles of the game of life are a very loose interpretation of the shamanic understanding of the nature of life.

Remember that we are sacrificing technical exactness for simplicity and easy accessibility to this important knowledge.

If we define life as a game with simple rules for winning and losing, then we can say that winning is being happy, being free to choose, being fulfilled, making a contribution, being of service, and walking the path of power. Losing would be failing to achieve any of these goals and feeling powerless and trapped with low self-esteem and no direction. As you have seen, winning this game of life requires power and energy. The sources of power and energy seldom come from a glamorous facade but rather from the hidden treasures that are often forgotten or overlooked. According to shamanic lore, without the power and energy to win, you will lose the game or be left in the dust while others survive and succeed.

Losing teaches you what not to do and shows you what does not provide power and energy, and so in losing you can continue to learn and still walk the path of power. This eventually will lead to winning provided that you learn well from your losses. You are free to choose how long it takes and how many times you repeat the same mistakes. As in all interesting games, there are obstacles and opponents in the way of winning. How you approach these obstacles has everything to do with the *kind* of power you have accumulated and whether or not you know how to use it well.

External, or visible, kinds of power are readily recognized in the everyday world of business and we are suggesting invisible forms of power are largely unrecognized and even unknown in the business world. The pursuit of this invisible kind of power is a high-risk operation with many potential pitfalls. Shamans know that the very power they seek can destroy them if they do not have sufficient discipline and awareness to handle it. This is not unlike the challenge of a rising young rock star or actor whose early success and fortune disastrously fuel their own self-destruction.

We will discuss the visible and invisible kinds of power further in a later chapter. For now let us concentrate more on the parallels between the shaman's world and the modern business world.

The Compelling Game of Business

Business is one of the most exciting games on the planet, right up there with the games of romance, athletic competition, raising a family, political ascendancy, and spiritual mastery. In fact, the game of business is an excellent microcosm of the larger game of life. We can apply everything in the shamanic rules of the game of life equally to the rules of the game of business. Thus, winning in business, too, has to do with how you approach the obstacles and the kind of power you choose to use in your pursuit of excellence.

Obstacles can either defeat or strengthen you. Your weaknesses can make you the hunted or they can teach you where your unrealized potential lies. Nothing could be truer in the world of business, where the competition easily exploits weakness but where one can also harness weakness to produce success. Avis, for example, knew that it could not beat Hertz as the number one car rental agency so they turned their weakness into a strength by billing themselves as number two. Being number two became a powerful selling strategy, something that worked in their favor and could not be used against them.

In the hardscrabble corporate game, what could be more exciting than to build a successful business, produce great products, market them everywhere, negotiate well, have excellent employees, and make a great deal of money along the way? That of course is the ideal, but many businesses fail financially, and even the ones that succeed often fail to produce happiness for their owners or employees. How many businesses actually conform to our definition of winning the game of life for everyone involved? Perhaps not as many as we would like to see. So, what is the core problem? The problem is that most people are playing the game using a manual that has crucial missing parts; it is similar to trying to run a seventh-generation software program using the manual that was created for the primitive first one.

What is needed is a manual that points out the obvious but often neglected truth. Shamans of the indigenous world are successful because they pay attention to the obvious and never lose sight of it. In the business world specialists are often called in to repair computers and other equipment only to discover that a unit was not plugged in or a cable had simply come loose. When we overlook the small but fundamental details in front of our faces because we are focusing on the large complexities, we work far below the optimum and are in danger of undermining the entire operation.

Business trainers continue to make fortunes teaching myriad strategies to succeed in this high-stakes game. They teach you important concepts like time management, putting first things first, how to handle stress, add value, create smart teams, motivate, and create an action plan. While these concepts are valuable, they are only as effective as the foundation from which you implement them. If you know nothing about the source of real power, then you will be unable to make the most effective use of these tools; they will simply remain good ideas but not active solutions.

Are you enjoying the game and winning from the shamanic frame of reference? Are you being outwardly successful but not enjoying the process that got you into your business or organization in the first place? If you are no longer enjoying the game, what would it take to get you back into your power? Selling your business? Changing how you approach it? Restructuring your relationship with it? Shifting your perspective and reframing it? Take a moment and attempt to answer these questions for yourself. You will find that the most accurate responses come immediately without second-guessing. Spend a little more time contemplating your responses after you have jotted them down. How are you going to get yourself back on track if you feel you have deviated from it?

SUMMARY

Important Concepts to Remember

- Life is a game of power.
- Business is a game of power.
- In the game of life and business, winning is being happy, free to choose, fulfilled.
- Losing is being frustrated and failing to achieve goals.
- Being successful requires the power and energy to manifest success.
- This power is often hidden and not easily seen.

Chapter 4

THE SHAMANIC FLOW
OF POWER

The good hunter acknowledges that there are superior forces within this universe which guide him as well as all other creatures. These forces dictate the circumstances of both life and death.

— Theun Mares, *Return of the Warriors: The Toltec Teachings*

Understanding the mysteries of life will alter how we think about organizations, management, and social change. Business, it turns out, can learn a great deal from nature.

— Richard Pascale, Mark Millemann, and Linda Gioja,
Surfing the Edge of Chaos

RULE I

All objects in the universe are following
the path of power.

A. Everything in the universe manifests the
amount of power it has gained thus far.

B. More powerful objects make it possible for

objects with less power to become more
powerful.

To say that you cannot manifest more power than
you have gained so far is to state the obvious, but those
seeking to manifest greater power too often overlook
this truth. A tree is only as big as it has grown until a
given moment and a bear is only as strong as it has
become. At this moment you have only the power you
have earned, no more and no less. No amount of wanting, hoping, or pretending will change this simple and
neutral fact. Therefore, you must match the level of
your current power with the power required for what
you want to accomplish to know whether you are powerful enough to tackle it. To overestimate your power
will cause problems and can even be catastrophic; to
underestimate it will not move you forward in any ben-
eficial way.

Shamans are critically aware of this natural law and
know they must act according to it if they want to survive. If they attempt to handle a challenge that requires
more power than they have, the result can be harmful
— it can even mean death — so they must be intensely
realistic and clear about where they stand. If a job is too
big or advanced for them, they refer it to a more accomplished shaman.

A shaman we met briefly in the Amazon region of
South America had the opportunity to come to the
United States to offer ceremonies and do some healing
work. The trip offered him the possibility of expanding

his work into another country and widening his reputation and success. However, a drinking problem that he had not yet conquered compromised his work. His trip to the United States, a test of his power, turned out to be a disaster because of his excessive drinking. Under the influence of alcohol he got involved sexually with women who were his patients, and he was forced to return home in disgrace. He had simply not yet accumulated enough power to overcome his problem and so could not meet the challenge he took on.

Just as students excel when tasks challenge but do not exceed their skill levels, you are most effective when you act with the power you have so far gained; to push too far ahead is to ensure failure. Business is generally no different in this respect, and although this simple shamanic rule appears obvious, businesses fail every day because they ignore it. A television commercial for an Internet service showed the staff of a start-up company eagerly watching the first sales of their product come in over the Internet. As they watch with unbridled enthusiasm and delight, the orders come in rapidly and begin to pile up. Suddenly they are overwhelmed with orders and their faces transform from excitement to dismay and then incredulity. Clearly they are unprepared to fill the huge number of orders and they despair over this new crisis they face. The ad demonstrates the power of the Internet service, but, for our purposes, it also warns of the need to be prepared for the dramatic outcomes of wielding power.

A shaman understands that the rule that everything

manifests only the power it has accumulated thus far holds a couple of important lessons. The first is that *bigger is not necessarily better.* A company wishing to grow will probably not find advantage in expanding in every direction with offers of widely disparate products. Perhaps it is better to stick with a line of products the company is known for and carefully and gradually develop them. The second lesson is that *impatience is a deadly obstacle to achieving power.* Trying to grow too fast and take on too much too quickly will lead to a stumble if not a precipitous fall. The path of power should be trod gradually and steadily in increments that can be assimilated and integrated productively.

The second sub-rule states that more powerful objects make it possible for objects with less power to become more powerful. We know that the sun provides energy to the earth in the form of light and heat, that the earth needs the sun to sustain life but the sun does not need the earth. A hair on your body depends on your body to sustain it but you do not need that one hair to sustain you. This relationship of more powerful to less powerful exists throughout the universe, from the largest objects to the smallest, from larger fields of energy to smaller fields, from higher frequencies to lower ones.

From our point of view, the solution to becoming powerful is actually rather simple. To become more powerful you must discover what is more powerful than you are and then spend time with it, absorbing some of its light, energy, and power. You have several options.

Options for Gaining Power

The first option is to simply look around you and notice who has power and who does not. Look at who has real power, not just the appearance of power. Spend time with some of those people who have power. Traditionally these people have been given various names like mentor, teacher, guide, and so on.

Corporations should look to see where their real power lies. No corporation or organization of any kind exists in isolation. For a business to produce it depends on suppliers and customers. If the suppliers are few then the business's growth is limited; if the suppliers are many then the business can develop strength. If the market is small or limited this curtails the growth of the business; if the market is large the business can become powerful.

This should be quite obvious, but what many businesspeople fail to realize is that the marketplace is where the power lies. The customer base needs to be bigger and more powerful than the business itself, and if it is, the shamanic rule can then manifest: more powerful objects make it possible for objects with less power to become more powerful.

The second option for gaining power is to look around you and notice what you depend on for your life. The truth is you depend on nature for life. It is important to spend time with aspects of nature: powerful waterfalls, forests, rivers, oceans, coasts, winds, deserts, animals, plants, sunsets, sunrises, and so on. We are not simply being sentimental environmentalists here; ancient traditions, mysticism, spiritual teachings, indigenous cultures, and shamans everywhere teach the same thing: *Power is in nature*. Without nature humans would not survive.

Nature is clearly more powerful than you are: Nature can exist without you but you cannot exist without it. You can choose to ignore this fact, but, in so doing, you will deny yourself access to a powerful source of energy. This is why shamans, who recognize nature's great power, spend a great deal of time outdoors, often just sitting or walking, absorbing, learning, and growing more powerful. Shamans make a point to greet the morning sun, absorb the noonday sun, witness the sunset, bathe in moonlight and starlight, climb trees to spend many hours in their branches, sit by waterfalls, lie on hot rocks, and experience nature in countless other ways.

In many organizations staff work all day in sterile environments without windows and devoid of natural beauty, and they are expected to thrive and become powerful. While the company may seem to prosper in terms of short-term profits, from our shamanic point of view, the staff are being slowly killed off because they are deprived of the great power of the natural environment, and this in turn will kill the company. Businesses that recognize the importance of the power of nature will thrive in the long run.

Here's the third option for gaining power: All shamanic traditions teach that the physical world depends on invisible dimensions, what they call a world of spirit. That spirit world, which consists of many dimensions and frequencies, is found within everything, including oneself. To become more powerful, we suggest you spend more time looking deeper within, because that is where the real power is. People who refuse to look inside themselves or who do not know how to look within are the most likely candidates for powerlessness or illusion. They are the ones most inclined to use external power inappropriately and eventually bring terrible consequences on themselves and others.

To begin looking deeply within, choose your form of meditation or contemplation. The form or style need not be an officially sanctioned one because contemplation can take place while running, walking, lying down, or sitting. Effective meditation means to quiet the mind for a time and to be still or silent. Power is waiting in the silence if you can get there; all it takes is time and practice.

We can unequivocally say that a business that provides its employees with the opportunity to go within has access to the greatest powers of the universe. We will discuss this concept much more in later chapters.

Exercise

Take a moment here to make a few lists, and answer a few questions.

First, list those people who are power sources for you or have been power sources in your life.

Second, list those places or things that nourish you

and make you feel more powerful when you spend time with them. Spend five or ten minutes being quiet and identifying where you feel your sources of power are at this time in your life: Family? Friends? Colleagues? Home? In philosophy? Spiritual life? This helps to become aware of external sources of power.

Finally, explore where you feel your power is located in your body: Heart? Head? Throat? Belly? Arms and hands? This helps to become aware of our internal sources of power.

SUMMARY
Important Concepts to Remember

- You cannot manifest more power than you have gained so far.
- You must match the level of your current power with the power required for what you want to accomplish to know whether you are powerful enough to tackle it.
- To overestimate your power can be catastrophic and to underestimate it will hamper your progress.
- In business bigger is not necessarily better.
- Impatience is a deadly obstacle to achieving power.
- More powerful objects make it possible for objects with less power to become more powerful.

- To become more powerful, you must discover what is more powerful than you are and then spend time with it.
- There are three options for gaining power: (1) observe who has real power; (2) sense what you depend on for your life; and (3) spend time looking deeper within, because that is where the real power is.

Chapter 5

THE FOUR SOURCES
OF POWER

Part of the magic of the experience lay in the sheer beauty of the setting: the breathtaking sight of the high mountains, the sweep of the sky, the panorama of the great valley. The beauty drives you out of the self for a moment — so that for a time the self is not. It's that indescribable feeling of coming together, time suspended; of being linked to the universe.

— Joseph Jaworski, *Synchronicity: The Inner Path of Leadership*

Your Silent Master Consciousness was born out of the infinite Life Force creating and animating the Universe. You exist as a part of the Universe; therefore It is the life force creating and animating you. It is the power that beats your heart. Because you are this Consciousness, whatever qualities the Life Force possesses, You possess also.

— Tae Yun Kim, *The Silent Master*

RULE 2

Power stems from four primary sources:
(1) inspiration; (2) simplicity;
(3) exchange; and (4) conception.

Monica: "Hey, Harry, welcome back! How was your vacation?"

Harry: "It was great! Fabulous! It was long overdue."

Monica: "You look great, really rested. Makes me realize I ought to get out too."

Harry: "Yeah, you don't know how badly you need it until you're there. It took me three whole days to relax into it. I finally realized I was on vacation. I was such a wreck when I left. Buurrnned out!"

Monica: "I know, it's hard to let down after working so hard. I can't believe how different you look. I'll bet you didn't want to come back. Was it hard to come in to the office?"

Harry: "No, not at all. By the end I felt ready to come back. I'm pretty energized, ready to go. I got what I needed."

Monica: "Where'd you go again, the Caribbean?"

Harry: "No, I was on the Big Island of Hawaii. We climbed up the volcano and spent some time on the seashore. What a perfect place! So beautiful! I just love the place, and so does Helen. Lot's of power there. So, how have things been around here, Monica?"

Monica: "Well, to tell you the truth, morale was a bit down last week, the focus a little scattered. I noticed a lot of people taking sick days or leaving early. You know, that's always a bad sign. But on Friday the prez decided to have a little get-together, you know just something simple, but it was really productive. We did a little acknowledgment of the production for this month, she gave us a pep talk, shared a story about her early days in the business. She also announced some changes. I'll fill you in. I think everyone felt a little better. It seemed that somehow the group vitality picked up after that. This week everyone is in a better mood, no absences that I can see, and the phones are ringing!"

Harry: "Well, looks like things are back on track here. I'm glad. I have a hard time getting away, but it seems like whenever I take a break, things work out for the better."

Monica: "Ain't it the truth. I always worry I can't afford to take the time, that things are going to fall apart, but they never do. Last time I took vacation time I came back to my biggest bonus check ever. By the way, do you remember that new designer paper that we were trying to market? I thought it was a loser and so did half the management. Well, the decision came down to put it on the shelf for now, not spend any more time or energy on it since it isn't what we are really in the business of selling. So, the good news is that we've decided to go ahead with that new printing operation that looks like it's going to be a real winner."

Harry: "All right! That's going to make things so much easier. That's great news."

Harry and Monica are managers in the marketing department of a major paper company boasting more than five hundred employees in their city alone. Their dialogue hints at the importance and effectiveness of understanding the sources of power available to anyone at any time; this understanding can lead to more harmony and productivity in the workplace.

WHERE DOES POWER COME FROM?

From our shamanic perspective, the universe is one vast field of power, an ocean of light, the primary source of all energy. This light creates structures and specific fields, some visible and others invisible to the human eye. Recognizing the limitlessness of knowledge in the universe, only a little of which science has decoded, a shaman understands that, rather than one, fixed reality, actually many dimensions overlap and coexist in the same space. These dimensions are specific frequencies of light that can be tuned in to like television stations.

We have observed that most of humanity is tuned to only one frequency or one agreed-upon channel out of the many that are available. While this might be practical for some purposes, the agreement limiting the experience of life to one channel can keep us from gaining solutions, having experiences, and accessing power in the other frequencies. Therefore, shamans learn to free themselves from this collective one-channel focus so they can access more frequencies and thus more power. A shaman can tap into parallel realities to gain access to solutions to problems, answers to questions, and resources unavailable in the agreed-upon reality.

Heraclitus, Leonardo da Vinci, Galileo, Socrates, Buddha, Jesus, Nikola Tesla, and even Thomas Edison were all masters at tapping into alternate realities to access powerful truths and abilities. All of them espoused the value of dreaming, the chief method of entering other frequencies.

According to indigenous wisdom, there is no shortage of power in the universe. At any given moment, no matter who you are or where you are or what state you feel yourself to be in, you have access to this stupendous, infinite resource. The ability to tap into a particular source of power requires changing your thinking and limited perception so that you can first recognize it and then being willing to do what it takes to access it, including changing the channel of awareness. Knowing what you will use your power for is also an important key to this process.

Many sources of power all around you can be accessed anytime. We can categorize all sources of power under these four groups: *inspiration, simplicity, exchange,* and *conception.* Some power sources, such as nature, fall into more than one group. You will find that any successful and powerful person, project, or business regularly taps into all four of these categories. In a later chapter where we discuss energizers and energy leaks, we will go into much greater detail about these four categories of power and describe how to both use the positive resources and avoid the negative activities that sap your power base.

1. Inspiration

We take inspiration to mean "lifting up and making accessible." Rising up and accessing new levels of awareness is one of the most important activities that shamans engage in. They dedicate themselves to spending much of their time lifting themselves out of confusion, chaos, dysfunction, and powerlessness to discover clarity, insight, knowledge, and power. Naturally, they must lift themselves up to help others rise up and gain access to higher powers as well.

Under the inspiration group of power sources are the subcategories of *beauty, truth, courage, humor, potential, completion,* and *change.* Every shaman we know and indigenous peoples from all over the world espouse the value of these forms of inspiration and actively pursue disciplines to master each form. They are vital to anyone desiring to be successful in business or any other aspect of life.

A lack of inspiration can cause depression, lethargy,

lack of motivation, lack of vision, and of course, a feeling of powerlessness, the death knell for success. To fail
to rise up to access wisdom and power is to remain in
the muck and mire where problems remain unsolved.
Emulating the shaman's search for inspiration is a must
for anyone seeking to become truly powerful and effective in business.

2. Simplicity

Simplicity means to be free of deceit and complexity, a state that shamans find essential on their journey
to becoming powerful leaders. In shaman's parlance,
the simpler the more powerful, and this is what the
great shaman Jesus meant when he stated, "In order to
enter the kingdom of heaven you must become again
as little children." The search for simplicity is truly
challenging in the context of modern business practices, and it seems to become more difficult every day.
For shamans, simplicity means to cut to the core of
issues, to let go of all nonessential information, and to
attend to the quality of information rather than to its
quantity.

The simplicity group of power sources includes
silence, focus, clarity, innocence, presence, decision, and,
interestingly, *death,* because to die to something means
to have no attachments to it and to take nothing of it
with you.

A lack of simplicity signifies the absence of an
important power source and causes chaos, confusion,

and ambivalence, among other undesirable experiences of powerlessness. Whenever anything becomes too complicated, whether plans, objectives, methodologies, or processes, the result is a loss of power rather than a gain.

3. Exchange

To exchange means to reciprocate, trade, barter, or interchange. All of these processes are action-oriented and demand contact with the world at large. Shamans value exchange because, without it, no learning, no teaching, and no access to the power available everywhere in the environment can occur. You cannot gain power or exercise it without some form of exchange.

Exchange is the third main power source that shamans use, a large category that includes anything that exchanges with anything else, any two parts that are in relationship to each other. A few important power sources in this category are *service, right working configurations or power groups,* and *all manner of relationships,* from partnerships to teacher-student agreements to supportive friendships and even enemies. In the area of relationships, *attention, acknowledgment, generosity, trust, vulnerability, love,* and *expression* are also included in this group.

A lack of exchange in your life will lead to a dark, lonely, and powerless place, characterized by despair, inertia, and withdrawal. A successful and powerful business has constant, active exchange both within the organization and with the suppliers and markets out-side its walls.

4. Conception

From shamans, we have learned that when we are conceived an explosion takes place, a blinding flash of light that becomes the foundation, the bank of power that we have to work with to develop into fully grown people. Conception is like a mainline of power from the source of the universe. Imagine that you are waiting in line to enter into a new country. An official reaches into a bag of money and pulls out a fistful of bills and hands it to each new entrant as seed money. Each fistful con-tains varying amounts but nevertheless an abundance of cash to make a start; some recipients will spend the money immediately, some will hoard it, some will give it away, and others will invest it wisely.

So, shamanically speaking, some start with more power, some with less, depending on the circumstances surrounding conception. But, no matter how much you start with, you always have plenty to work with. Even the least powerful conception generates more energy than can ever be used. How you use your power is what counts in your life. Sadly, as in the example above, many people choose to squander it through addictions, resent-ment, victimization, arrogance, impatience, and greed. Some merely try to hold on to it without investing it. Others put it right to work building a growing founda-tion of power to operate from throughout life.

We have observed that, the quality of the conception of anything — a human being, a project, a business, or a community — determines the amount of power that generates from it. Included in this category of sources of power are *birth, origin, imagination,* and *idea.*

THE FOUR SOURCES OF POWER AT WORK

In the earlier example of Harry and Monica, Harry was lacking inspiration prior to his vacation. For whatever reason, he couldn't tap into his power sources. By taking time off, changing his scenery, and reconnecting with the beauty found in nature, Harry tapped the power source of inspiration through beauty and became energized. Another source that Harry tapped into was power through simplicity via the silence of the mountain, which also enabled him to focus simply on the task in front of him, to put one foot in front of the other until he reached the top.

Meanwhile, back at the office, Monica describes the actions taken at work to tap into the power source of exchange through (1) acknowledgment of the staff at the gathering and (2) better communication. Another power source tapped into was simplicity through the decision to let go of the designer paper being tested on the market. The power source of inspiration came into play with (1) the courage it took to make that decision and (2) the vision connected with the new printing operation. Developing the new plant opened up the power source of conception and birth.

Later in this book we will go more deeply into the management of these sources of power and discuss when and how to use them as sources. We will also take a good look at the different ways you lose power and the experiences, situations, and aspects that contribute to power loss.

Exercise

What activities do you find most inspiring at this time in your life? Jot a few of these things down.

What works well in your life and at work because of its simplicity? What could become simpler than it is now?

What are the principal sources of exchange that you find nourish you and empower you at this time?

What is emerging, growing, being conceived inside you right now? Where does this emerging vision want to go? How does it want to be expressed?

SUMMARY
Important Concepts to Remember

- A shaman can tap into parallel realities to gain access to solutions to problems, answers to questions, and resources unavailable in the agreed-upon reality.
- According to indigenous wisdom, there is no shortage of power in the universe.

- You always have access to this stupendous, infinite resource.
- The ability to tap into a particular source of power requires changing your thinking and limited perception so that you can first recognize power and then being willing to do what it takes to access power, including changing the channel of awareness.
- Power stems from four primary sources: (1) inspiration; (2) simplicity; (3) exchange; and (4) conception.

Chapter 6

THE NEUTRALITY OF POWER

Do you have a guiding vision for your life, and how do you build the personal power to follow that vision to its fulfillment?

— Tom Pinkson, *The Flowers of Wiricuta*

RULE 3

Power in itself is neutral. It is neither good nor bad. It just is. How you manage it determines the positive or negative consequences for you and others.

Since power is neutral, what you do with it determines the positive or negative consequences for you and others. What we are suggesting is that you cannot

alter the essential nature of power based on whether
you like it or not, just as the sky above is not influenced
by whether you find it beautiful, oppressive, threatening, or anything else. The sky is what it is no matter
what your vote. How you perceive power determines
whether you enjoy it or hate it, feel in charge of it or its
effects, or use it well or poorly.

The more you resist your own power, the greater
the chances you will perceive negative expressions of it.
For example, when someone is afraid of their own
power, it often shows up in nightmares as monsters
and threatening figures. Perceiving power negatively
also happens when you resist power in others or in natural phenomena.

A number of years ago we were deep in the desert of
central Mexico attending an overnight ceremony with a
group of Huichols. It was November, and the temperature plummeted at sunset to below freezing. The winds
picked up and began to blow hard, creating a serious
windchill factor that froze our hands, feet, and faces. We
surrounded a tiny fire that guttered and blew about in
the harsh wind, providing little if any heat to our back-
sides facing the relentless desert wind. It was only 9:00
P.M. and already we were miserable, wondering how we
would make it through the night without freezing to
death. Heavily bundled in down jackets, wool hats, and
boots, we observed that the Huichols wore sandals without socks and were dressed only in thin, decorated
cotton shirts and pants. We were amazed at their apparent disregard for the conditions as they laughed and carried on as if a warm sun were shining.

We saw from their example that you could generate enough energy to enjoy the night and be quite comfortable. They clearly had the power to do this and were in no way resisting the elements howling about us. Although the ground frosted over and the wind never let up, we gradually began to warm enough to doff our heavy jackets, relax, and enjoy the ceremony. By morning we had learned a valuable lesson; without resistance, we accomplished something that we would have thought quite impossible.

The lesson we learned was that the more you resist the power of nature, the more you are likely to experience its power negatively. This does not alter the nature of its power, only how you perceive it.

Our Huichol friends were powerful because they did not resist the world around them. Time and again we observed how cheerful and happy they seemed, no matter the conditions confronting them. They took no notice of freezing temperatures as they walked for miles in sandals with no socks. Traveling by crowded, noisy bus for twenty-four hours while sleeping sitting up was not a problem for them. Standing in line for hours in a government building in 100-degree heat with no air conditioning did not dampen their spirits one bit. They were always fully present, accepting, enjoying, and being with whatever was. By comparison we were soft, critical, and lazy.

Resisting the power in others at work likewise creates powerlessness and misery, whereas studying it and being with it produce a far different result. Mandy's corporate experience is a good example:

Mandy couldn't stand working for the new supervisor assigned to her division in the large pharmaceutical company where she was employed. Every day she felt more powerless to express herself under this domineering chief, and each day he appeared to have more power over her. One day after a particularly rancorous meeting with him, she had an important insight. She realized that it didn't matter to him whether she liked him or not. She also realized that while she hated aspects of his dominant personality that reminded her of her stepfather, he was knowledgeable and good at getting things done in a division that had previously been unproductive. She determined that as long as she had to work with him, she was going to learn as much as possible by observing what he did to accomplish his goals. With this understanding and new intention, she instantly felt empowered, and the positive results were readily apparent. In a rather short time he was transferred to another trouble spot, and she was promoted to become the division head herself.

Often we discover that our clients harbor a great fear of power despite the fact that they clearly hold positions of power within their corporations. This fear of the power they potentially wield amounts to nothing less than resistance to what is.

One of our clients was a senior vice president who had just been made head of the organizational development department of a major corporation. She was deeply suspicious of and uneasy with the notion that she occupied a position of power and influence. Carol seemed to want to create the illusion for herself that everyone was the same and she was no more powerful than anyone else, including all the managers who reported to her. Because of this she was having difficulty with some of those managers; they didn't listen to her or act upon her suggestions and guidance. Our first task with Carol was to get her to recognize her negative attitude about power and her great fear of being the one to use it and potentially abuse it. She could easily identify that these fears stemmed from her own experience with an abusive and mentally ill father.

With coaching she understood that power was not inherently evil but rather a powerful tool she could use in a positive way to revamp the department and make it an effective asset for hundreds of employees. As she began to perceive the inherent neutrality of power itself, she became more effective at using it according to her own value system. Eventually she became the most valued assistant to the CEO of the corporation, who relied on her judgment and suggestions for all major policy decisions.

Desperately wanting power is also a form of resistance, because when you are in this state, you fear that you don't have it. You are resisting not having it, and therefore are not neutral.

What you resist you give power to, so you create the illusion of being powerless. When you can be with the current conditions and simply acknowledge them, you pave the way for changing conditions and the arrival of new levels of power.

Here's an example:

Ahmed was intensely unhappy with his slow rise up the managerial ladder at the four-star hotel where he supervised the service staff. Each day he arrived home complaining to his wife that he was being held up by the vice president. The more he fretted over his situation, the more powerless he became. Eventually it even affected his relationship with his wife, and he withdrew from her, creating further problems at home, his one base of support.

When we discussed this situation with Ahmed, we saw that his unhappiness stemmed from his unrealistic expectations. He had set an unrealistic internal timetable for himself to attain certain goals, and he had created high expectations that were frustrated with each day that passed. In short, he was not at all neutral about his current level of power, and his expectations were constantly throwing him into the future and preventing him from enjoying himself.

We suggested that he let go of all expectations and his timetable for three months. During that time he was to forget about advancement and concentrate instead on what he liked about his current work. With discussion, he created a list of fifteen things he liked about his present job. These included such duties as interviewing prospective staff members, attending a weekly meeting with his staff, and participating in an in-service training program in management skills. We suggested that he spend his time enjoying as many of these fifteen things as possible on a daily basis.

Fortunately he was game and agreed to the process. Within a week he had received compliments from his supervisor and several staff members praised him for being a good boss to them. Within a month he was promoted.

When Ahmed let go of his resistance, he could be with what was enjoyable about his work, and that was the key to change in his position of power. From resistance he could not gain power, but by making the pursuit of power less important, he actually secured more of it. The simplicity of this process — and its great effects — truly amazed him.

Exercise

Take your notebook and write down the following statement: *"Every aspect of power is easy and comfortable for me."* Now jot down the first ten thoughts, feelings, and attitudes that arise in you in response to reading the statement. Don't mull it over too much; just write the first things that come to mind.

Next consider how you feel about exercising the power you have been given. How are you at being reprimanded or accepting criticism? How are you at reprimanding an employee? At firing someone? How are you at issuing orders? Following orders? How are you at initiating a truthful but difficult conversation with someone? How do you feel about the fact that others have more power than you in the workplace? How do you feel about the fact that you have more power than others in the workplace?

SUMMARY

Important Concepts to Remember

- The essential nature of power is not altered based on whether you like it or not.
- The more you resist your own power, the greater the chances you will perceive negative expressions of it.
- The more you resist the power in others or in natural phenomena, the more you will perceive negative expressions of it.

Chapter 7

THE PROPER TIMING OF POWER

If learning and change are truly our intent, a slower, more demanding and more deliberating approach is required. We have to value struggle over prescription, questions over answers, tension over comfort, and capacities over needs and deficiencies.

— Peter Block, *Flawless Consulting: A Guide to Getting Your Expertise Used*

The error of man is to seek explanations which substantiate his view of the world. The unknown cannot be explained in this way. As a result all explanations turn into a matter of blind faith or superstition.

— Theun Mares, *Return of the Warriors: The Toltec Teachings*

RULE 6

Power can be hunted and gained in ways similar to the rules of the hunt in the natural environment.

FOUR APPROACHES TO TIMING YOUR POWER BID

As you face new challenges each day, you constantly have choices about how you are going to meet them. Most people tend to go unconscious while making these choices, without actually realizing what is at stake. Being conscious and aware of what you are doing is the first step to making the correct choices and making them from a place of power.

As you shall see, acting from a position of power rests on the firm foundation of *paying attention*. Without attention during a hunt, a mountain lion can never know when to spring to action, when to wait for a more opportune moment, what direction to begin the charge, and what the obstacles might be. Without attention the lion will never eat.

Backing away from a challenge when you are not ready to embrace it is a sign of wisdom and an act of power that leaves you with the option to fight or dance another day. When faced with prostate cancer and a difficult divorce, Mayor Giuliani of New York City agonized over his campaign against Hillary Clinton for the senate. After evaluating his situation, he wisely bowed out of the race to attend to his overall health. Although to some this would appear to be an admission of failure, it was actually an act of personal power. He chose a course that would more likely allow him to heal and live longer over a choice that would have presented him with some difficult challenges, and possibly even would have killed him. Likewise, an executive coach we know prudently opted for a few months more of training supervision prior to working independently with a new method of consulting.

On the other hand, delaying facing a challenge when you are ready because you chronically underestimate yourself is a loss of power as well.

Jack, a forty-year-old hospital administrator, hated his job and felt deep inside that he would be much happier in the field of human resources. Although he was personally and professionally well qualified to make the shift and was encouraged to do so from many other people, he simply could not find the confidence to take the risk. Instead, he lingered in his uncomfortable position until the hospital, facing hard times, began reducing staff. He survived cut after cut, but instead of reading the writing on the wall, he held on to his position, fearing it was the only one he could get. Eventually reality caught up with him and he was let go. Instead of acting from a position of power, he contracted and supported his fears until they were realized.

There is a saying that *timing is everything*. Knowing the right timing for bidding for the next level of power is crucial. One of the ways to know that the timing and circumstances are right is to experience a level of ease and effortlessness that should accompany any bid for power. In a bid with right timing, everything seems to fall into place, doors open, and support comes from many different sources. One might still experience a "stretch," a test, but most likely enthusiasm, excitement, a sense of accomplishment, and acknowledgment and support from others will accompany the bid.

Many examples illustrate bidding for power in different settings in our society. Take the educational system with its levels of grades, tests, diplomas, graduations. Moving through the levels of responsibility and knowledge within this system is a recognized way of bidding for power and achieving it in increments. If you took a ten-year-old and placed them in a high school class, mentally and emotionally they would not be ready for this bid for power and they would be doomed to fail. For the same reason, you would not expect a twelve- or thirteen-year-old to be ready for the responsibility of taking care of a family or of living on their own.

Because of the heavy pressure to win at all costs and the extreme competitive atmosphere in much of the business world today, managers can make extremely unwise decisions in their mad grope for greater power.

Against all expert advice, the CEO of a fast-growing media company wanted to beat the competition by opening a second facility and warehouse on the East Coast. He experienced great success, market share, and sales figures, and he became greedy and impatient for more. Without allowing enough time for this foundation to anchor itself, he stretched resources to the limit, rationalizing an arrogant can-do attitude, and went for broke on his power bid. The market took a sudden downturn, and his project was left incomplete and underfunded. The whole system was in chaos, and the result was an unmitigated disaster. The company stock plummeted and the board of directors removed him from his position.

Had he waited for the right timing, which would have shown itself to him if he were patient, the project would have succeeded. In business, ill-timed expansion is common, and the lessons learned through failure are significant.

On the other hand, correctly bidding for power when you are ready is an act of supreme power. Like a lion stalking its prey, you wait and watch, maintaining your reserves until the exact moment when, with the least effort and the greatest speed, you bring your quarry down successfully.

A client of ours that has a small chain of hair and skin care salons shared her story of appropriate power bids over the last ten years. She started out in a salon owned by someone else and worked as long as was necessary to establish a reputation, form a strong base of clients, learn as much as she could about the business, and most important, save up some money. Her first bid for power was to open a small salon of her own, a one-person operation with no extras except the sale of a few products. Her second bid for power was to move her salon into a larger space, which she did only after two years of building up her clientele to the point of having a consistent waiting list and bookings for a month in advance. At the new location, she added a part-time receptionist and leased space to two other hairdressers. After consistently brisk business and three more years of maintaining a stellar reputation and building an even greater client base, the next bid for power was to add another service requested by her clientele, skin care. This required more education, some remodeling, the use of added resources, the addition of employees, and a marketing effort. The expansion was successful because certain ingredients and criteria for a bid for power were met.

After another year, one of the employees in the salon approached our client with the idea of opening a second salon in a neighboring town. The two of them planned this expansion very carefully, making sure that the employee thoroughly learned the nature of the business. Upon opening the second location, this employee, who had been a hairdresser in the first salon, became the manager of the second salon with an increased salary and a percentage of the profits — so this move was a successful bid for power by both parties. Today our client has five salons, all opened in the same way with everyone involved successfully making their bids for more power.

In the success story of the salon owner, the bids for power always included the following necessary ingredients: knowledge, experience, resources, integrity, and support. She continued her education in the field as needed, allowed the time necessary for building experience, made sure the resources were available, operated consistently out of integrity with all involved, and had the support of her clientele, who acknowledged her bid for power.

With regard to power, then, you have four options:

1. You can reject making a bid for power because

you correctly assess that you are not ready, you lack a key ingredient, or the timing isn't right, and thus maintain your power in your present situation.

2. You can hide from challenges and opportunities that would give you more power because your self-esteem is low, you mistrust your intuition, and your unfounded fears keep you from the bid even though many of the ingredients are there. This will cause you to lose some of your power.

3. You can arrogantly and impatiently take on challenges when you are not ready, when you lack the ingredients, and thus suffer the consequences, which inevitably lead to a setback and major power loss.

4. You can watch, learn, and wait until you recognize the ingredients are in place and you are ready to take on new opportunities. This way you gain power in increments, even though you may make minor mistakes along the way.

Exercise

1. Think of a least one time that you correctly backed down from an opportunity because you were clearly aware that you were not ready to take on the responsibility it required.

2. Think of a time when you lost an opportunity to become more powerful because you incorrectly underestimated yourself at the time.

3. Think of a time when you took on more than you were ready for and more than you could handle and the results were a loss of power for you.

4. Think of a time when you correctly waited and patiently bided your time until you were ready to take on more power and the results were excellent.

SUMMARY

Important Concepts to Remember

- You can hunt and gain power in ways similar to the rules of the hunt in the natural environment.
- Acting from a position of power rests on the firm foundation of *paying attention*.
- Timing is everything. Knowing the right timing for bidding for the next level of power is crucial.
- There are four approaches to timing:

  1. Reject making a bid for power when you are truly not ready.
  2. Hide from challenges and opportunities out of fear.
  3. Arrogantly and impatiently take on challenges when you are not ready.
  4. Watch, learn, wait, and pay attention until it is the right time to bid for power.

Chapter 8

BIDDING FOR POWER

There is a superior and guiding force for all creation. This force is true power, or spirit.

— Ken Eagle Feather, *A Toltec Path*

The reputation of power is power.

— Thomas Hobbes, quoted in *Hardball* by Christopher Matthews

RULE 4

The path of power is expensive:
There is always a price to pay for real power.

There is always a price to pay for real power. You may bid for power at any time and as often as you wish, but you will be tested to see if you are ready and deserving. A bid for power is a personal decision to acquire more power by taking on a challenge. By definition, a bid for more power is a risk, a stretch, an exciting prospect. The game of life has infinite opportunities to gain power; indeed, you can scarcely avoid accumulating power on a daily basis if you so desire.

Babies bid for power when they scream to call someone to pick them up. Toddlers bid for power when they rise up on their legs and take a shaky step or two. A child bids for power by climbing a fence to roam the neighborhood to explore or search for friends. A teenager bids for power by asking someone for a date. An adult bids for power by interviewing for a job. The examples are endless.

The important thing to understand is that a bid for power must come from within yourself. If you are following someone else's agenda for what is best for you, if someone else manipulates or shoves you forward, then you are not establishing a legitimate bid for power. Rather, under these circumstances, you may be experiencing their bid for power carried out through you, but in an ineffective, unhelpful, and perhaps even harmful way. A good illustration of this is the child actor placed under so much pressure to succeed by an ambitious parent that the child turns to drugs or alcohol and destroys any opportunities for success.

From our perspective, everyone should know some important rules regarding bidding for power. Many of these rules are obvious but are nevertheless usually ignored, even by those who should know better. People ignore these rules for two main reasons: (1) many distractions in our lives fill our minds with constant, endless thought and, (2) in the workplace, the games and politics of the company so often induce us to enter a waking and yet unconscious trance.

A shaman makes it a point to remember these rules and be absolutely aware of them at all times when making a bid for power. When we remember these rules, we free ourselves from worries about failure.

THE SHAMANIC RULES OF BIDDING FOR POWER

In the game of life anyone can bid for power at any time. The power may be the visible, external kind such as a promotion, the expansion of an existing business, opening a new business, entering into a partnership, or making a large acquisition. Or it may be a bid for the invisible kind of power, such as developing greater intuition, more certainty and self-assurance, or even a greater sense of well-being.

Bidding for either kind means that you are willing to take on responsibilities at a higher level of risk. In a choice to run for public office, for example, some of the risks are the vulnerability to public criticism and scrutiny and the elevated stress in one's personal life. When you request a raise, you are bidding for a higher sense of self-assurance and self-worth, and you are also willing to perhaps take on a larger workload or be ultimately more responsible for a project. If you initiate a large growth step for your corporation or open up new markets, you may risk your credibility if the project doesn't work out. You open yourself up to greater criticism in failure, and yet of course to higher praise if you meet with success. You need to be able to handle both. Therefore, in addition to having the necessary ingredients discussed earlier, you must meet certain other conditions should you decide to make a bid for power.

1. You must be completely ready at a variety of levels or the bid for power will result in humiliating defeat. Bidding for power when you are not ready produces negative consequences for yourself and others associated with you; it can have an unexpected blow back or boomerang effect. Instead of becoming more powerful, you are likely to end up falling off the ladder.

Questions for Business

- Should you expand your operations when you are undercapitalized?
- Should you announce a new product before it has undergone quality control?
- Should you ask for a promotion if you are not fulfilling your present job responsibilities?

2. You must be able to identify when you are ready. Being ready does not mean being perfect or being totally without fear. Being ready means being able to adapt and to learn the rules of the game as you play and to continue in this manner as the rules change. When a bobcat commits to the chase, it commits to going nearly anywhere, over logs, into a stream, or down a hole. Are you ready to see the chase through, regardless of where it takes you?

Questions for Business

- Should you ask for a raise when you are doing more than everyone else in your department but are fearful of going to your supervisor?
- If you have done a great job of adapting to your present position, should you request a promotion to the level of a manager even though you do not know everything that will be thrown at you in that position?
- Should you go to the boss with a new product design even though you are not sure what the reaction will be?

3. **You must be prepared psychologically, physically, emotionally, and spiritually.** You must be physically capable of undergoing the stress accompanying a bid for power. A sick tiger does not hunt successfully. You must be reasonably healthy psychologically. You must be mature enough emotionally. You must be adaptable. You must have developed an awareness of yourself to the degree that you are spiritually prepared for the consequences of winning or losing.

Questions for Business

- Should you take on new managerial responsibilities even though you are on a high dose of tranquilizers or heart medication?
- Should you aggressively promote a new marketing campaign even though you have recently had quadruple bypass surgery?
- Should you represent the union at the yearly meeting even though you have been crying yourself to sleep every night over your recent divorce?

4. You must have knowledge, experience, and perseverance. Once you commit to something, stick with it and follow it as far as you can. With perseverance, knowledge and experience will come.

Questions for Business

- Should you apply for department director even though you have no prior experience in that field?
- Should you move into a new position even though you aren't comfortable with some of the job requirements and have been on the job for only two months?
- Are you willing to see a tough project through to completion even if you are discouraged at times?

5. **You must also understand the true nature of the risks** that you are taking and the risks you are asking others to take alongside you. Failure to consider the degree of risk can be disastrous. A lion always carefully observes its prey and calculates the risks before springing to the attack.

Questions for Business

- Are you willing to risk your colleagues' and co-workers' disapproval when you are promoted to be their new supervisor?
- Is building the new facility going to jeopardize the survival of the firm?
- If the new idea fails, how many jobs will be lost? Will you still be employed?
- Is merging with a larger corporation in everyone's best interest or does it just look good statistically?
- If it fails, are you willing to accept the consequences?

6. **When you bid for greater power, you must, paradoxically, have arrived at a state where you do not personally care, from an ego point of view, whether you achieve it this time or not.** You must be prepared to bid again and again until you succeed. If you are ego invested and demand that you succeed now or else, you are asking for trouble. Nor can your bid for power be a personal test to see if you are intelligent enough,

attractive enough, or cunning enough. These agendas will distract you from the goal and cause you to fail.

A fox is not ego invested in whether it is smart enough to catch its prey. The hunt either succeeds or does not. The fox either eats or it doesn't. If it fails to catch its prey, the fox merely hunts again and again relentlessly until it eats. The fox is not trying to prove anything to itself, nor should you.

Questions for Business

- Should you ask the boss for a raise just to find out what the boss thinks of you?
- Will your self-esteem be shattered if the committee does not accept your new product design.
- Are your prepared to reapply for a management position even though you were passed over the first time?

7. **You must act without hesitation** when you have assessed that you are ready to bid for power. You must commit yourself completely, like the falcon diving for prey. At two hundred miles per hour, you are committed.

Questions for Business

- Should you decide not to offer a product after you have announced to the public its imminent availability?

- Should you change your mind about disman-
  tling a department after you have let go of
  most the staff?
- Should you dither over whether to fire the
  chief financial officer even though she has
  already lost credibility with the board of
  directors?

These questions may seem simplistic, and as you
read over them the answers may seem obvious, but in
the real world of complex systems you may lose your
perspective and clarity. The reality is that foolish decisions and actions are offered as answers to questions
like these every day in the business world, and the
results are often catastrophic. The solution is to be
aware of the shamanic rules related to bidding for
power and to play by them at all times.

You'll pay a price for a step up in power but suffer
a severe consequence for bragging about power when
you have not earned it.

The Cost of Announcing the Achievement of Power Too Soon

Arrogantly announcing that you have attained a
specific level of inner or outer power before you actually have is a common mistake that can lead to negative consequences. Prematurely claimed success has
been the downfall of many a power player. In ancient
China, if the emperor fell ill, physicians were called in
to care for him. If they succeeded in their healing

ministrations and the emperor recovered, they gained
prestige and financial rewards. If the emperor got
worse or died, they could be executed. Talk about consequences! In the eighteenth century a number of
Native American medicine men were murdered when
they failed to cure members of their tribe who fell ill
with measles. A shaman who tries to undo the curse
of a more powerful sorcerer can endanger their own
life and the lives of their family as well. In the world
of shamans and healers, consequences for failure can
be extreme, and this is why they place such great
emphasis on being truly ready. This is also why they
warn against the foolhardiness of making promises
they cannot keep or of egotistically boasting of powers
that they do not have yet.

In the world of business the consequences are of
course not nearly as extreme. Usually the worst that
can happen is a loss of prestige, reputation, finances, or
position. Compared to curses and execution, these consequences are relatively mild, and you can usually
bounce back. However, examples in business of boasting "done deals" before the right time are many — a
company or individual announces a successful merger
or acquisition that is not yet fully signed and agreed
upon by all parties; a real estate deal is not finalized by
all parties involved but forms the basis for a business
expansion; an advertised inflated market share of a
franchise is not yet established. Such claims are usually
ego driven and can greatly interfere with the success of
a power bid.

Exercise 1: Failed Bids for Power

Almost everyone has a personal example of a fool-hardy bid for power made when they were not yet ready. Have you made mistakes of this kind and suffered the consequences? Make a list of all your most embarrassing miscalculations, especially ones where you announced success too soon. Grab a piece of paper and write down as many ill-chosen bids for power as you can remember. Carefully study the circumstances and your attitude at the time you made the fateful decision and try to answer all of the following questions:

What were you thinking? What were you feeling? What did you think you were going to gain? Whose information were you operating from that led you to your decision? What did you learn from announcing victory or success before you secured it? How did you lose power as a result? Did you in fact gain anything?

Exercise 2: Upcoming Bids for Power

Contemplate the following questions and attempt to answer them as honestly as possible:

What is the next bid for power that is up for you at work? Are you ready? How will you know when you are ready? How can you prepare yourself to be ready? What will you have to sacrifice to become ready? What are the risks involved in your bid for power? Are you prepared to take them? How invested are you in the outcome? How devastated will you be if you fail? When is it time to act without hesitation?

SUMMARY

Important Concepts to Remember

- Rules of bidding for power:

  1. Be ready or suffer humiliating defeat.
  2. Know when you are ready.
  3. Be prepared psychologically, physically, emotionally, and spiritually.
  4. Have knowledge, experience, and perseverance.
  5. Understand the nature of the risks.
  6. Have no ego investment in gaining power.
  7. Act without hesitation.

- Never announce a gain of power before you have achieved it.

Chapter 9

THE PRICE OF POWER

Knowledge is ever greater and more powerful than man. To walk the path of knowledge is to fight for survival; therefore if you come to this path to learn, then you must be prepared to fight as if your life depended on it.

— Theun Mares, *Return of the Warriors: The Toltec Teachings*

Relentless discomfort sharpens the edge of action and reveals further possibilities.

— Richard Pascale, Mark Millemann, and Linda Gioja, *Surfing the Edge of Chaos*

RULE 4 CONTINUED

The path of power is expensive:
There is always a price to pay for real power.

Now we're ready to go more deeply into Rule 4: There is always a price to pay for real power. You may bid for power at any time and as often as you wish, but you will be tested to see if you are ready and deserving.

We have learned repeatedly from our teachers and from our own experience that bidding for power, whether at the visible or invisible level, always comes with a price. In terms of power there is no such thing as a free lunch, just as it is in the way of nature. The consequence of becoming a great river is no longer being a small stream. The result of becoming an adult grizzly bear is the loss of being a cub. Nature's assessment for becoming a tree is forfeiture of being the seed. In the natural environment these fees and costs go unquestioned. We accept and understand them at the deepest levels.

Humans, however, have developed strange concepts with regard to life's natural exchange system. Only humans think they can cheat the process, get something for nothing, obtain the goods without paying the price. Many people believe they can bid for power without paying any price whatsoever — perhaps this explains the huge popularity of lotteries, game shows, and gambling, which promise to make someone a multimillionaire with a mere spin of the wheel or a quick roll of the dice.

Another great cultural fantasy is that more money, influence, fame, success, and visibility will be a huge relief and will bring happiness and freedom from all suffering. Most people never project their thoughts beyond achieving their immediate goal, so they fail to note the price tag on the goal.

The shamanic rule again is that there is always a price to pay for such sudden gains, rises in popularity, affluence, and influence. The price may not be apparent; many of life's experiences do not come with an obvious or fixed price tag attached to them. They give the appearance of being free, like a golden apple just waiting to be plucked. In fact, more often than not the price of power is hidden, mysterious, coming due later like a debt that is revealed only over time.

From our understanding, this was the real meaning behind the tale of Adam and Eve and the Garden of Eden. If they were going to eat of the fruit of knowledge, then there was going to be a price. Was this a bad thing? We would say no, it wasn't: They chose to play the game of life, and that game had a price. What was the price? Simple: They sacrificed their own comfort level — and that is the price a shaman must never forget. To gain power, to grow and stretch, is an uncomfortable process and much will have to be sacrificed along the way. There is no free lunch. To become truly powerful is never a comfortable process.

In our perspective, the bid for outer forms of power like wealth and influence often carries the price of money and the investment of time. Bidding for this visible kind of power is fraught with pitfalls unless you have accumulated enough inner power to carry it through with integrity and impeccability. The temptation will be to become greedy and maybe even to cheat to get more, better, faster. If you choose to cheat, then the price includes losing your own integrity and impeccability. Without integrity and impeccability, you lose your invisible power and become weak.

Our Huichol shaman teacher once told us these chilling words: "If you do not keep your word, if you think you can get away with things because no one is there to catch you, if you think you can lie and cheat, then you are a fool. Behaving without integrity is like allowing thieves and murderers to rampage through your house!"

Since many people do not know about inner power, they put themselves at tremendous risk, bidding for visible power without having created any foundation. No wonder they so often crash and burn.

Great numbers of people in the business community have been brought down in disgrace because of greed, loss of integrity, and attempts to cheat in the game. From the shamanic perspective to cheat is pure stupidity because the game of power is absolutely ruthless. The consequences will be horrendous — and there will be consequences. Playing with outer power without developing inner power is a blueprint for disaster.

Bidding for inner power costs time and energy, and costs even more in terms of sacrificing long-held beliefs and attitudes. Inner power is even more difficult to handle than outer, visible power. If you bid for inner power, you will always be tested to see how well you do with it.

TESTS AND INITIATIONS

Shamanically speaking, when your bid for power succeeds, your success is always acknowledged by an initiation of some form. Initiations at both the inner and outer levels mark increasing levels of power. Many visible increases in power come with formal, culturally accepted initiations. These initiations pale in comparison to the scale of inner initiations that usually bring one face to face with what they fear the most. Bouts with extreme emotional discomfort usually accompany inner initiations.

Outer initiations come in the forms of societal rites of passage such as graduations, licenses, promotions, financial awards, and privileges. These are important because they give legitimacy to a new rank in society. While they establish a person's right to move up the ladder, it is up to him or her to prove worthiness in the long run.

Here's an example of one of José's experiences with test and initiation:

Upon completing my course work for my doctoral studies, I had to take a series of written and oral exams before I could then complete my dissertation. I aced all the exams except I failed statistics, my nemesis. To make matters worse, I had a rather negative feeling toward the statistics instructor, whose job it was to grade the exam. We'd had a rocky relationship from the beginning; the instructor treated me like I was incompetent and I had very little respect for the instructor, sensing that he was dishonest.

The next exam was scheduled for six months later, and I studied like mad to prepare for it. I got tutoring and learned statistics better than ever before. The exam date finally arrived, I took the exam, and then waited the six weeks to hear the results. Again I failed.

I was beside myself with grief, anxiety, and anger. I had to wait another six months. If I did not pass it the third time, I could never take it again and I would fail to receive my doctorate, even though I had completed all the course work and was well on my way to completing my dissertation. Again I studied, received tutoring, and prepared in every known possible way. I enlisted friends to pray for me. I visualized passing with flying colors and worked with affirmations to improve my attitude. I pursued hypnosis to be able to relax during the exam and bring up the right information.

The week before the exam I went out to the country for a couple of days to be alone in nature and just relax. Over and over again when I checked inside, I received the message that all was well and I would pass the exam. As if in confirmation, I observed, as I walked to a lookout, a hawk fly close over my head and circle several times. I felt confident I would pass.

The date arrived and I took the exam, feeling good about my answers. Again I waited, and when I opened the results with bated breath, I was horrified. With deep shock I read that I had failed for the third and last time. It was signed by the dreaded instructor. There were no notes on it, no indications why I had failed or which problems I had answered wrong. I was plunged into a nightmare of despair, feeling grave doubts about all the signs and messages I had received. For several days I was in a kind of stupor. Then mysteriously in the mail there arrived another manila envelope, this one containing another copy of my exam with the statement that I had passed, and signed by the dean of students. I never questioned this second letter. I went on to receive my doctorate, never knowing exactly what had happened, although I suspect that the dean had reviewed my test and decided to override my enemy instructor.

A year later I received the news in an official bulletin that the instructor had had his psychological practitioner's license revoked for fraud. It was not surprising news to me; I had a feeling the instructor's attitude would lead to a major problem of some kind.

What can be gleaned from this difficult experience of initiation?

1. Tests and initiations for power can appear in the form of ordinary events such as academic exams, interviews, and applications for new positions.
2. You know a test of your power has come when seemingly inexplicable obstacles are in your path and you have to dig ever deeper into your resources to handle them.
3. During a power test you will probably feel out of control at times and frustrated at your inability to change events that take place around you.

4. During a power test you might meet with a
   antagonist who makes life difficult for you.

5. A power test will always come with a secret
   helper or ally. You will not know when or
   where or how they will appear, but we advise
   you never to refuse or question their help.

6. A power test will often take you to your
   absolute limit of endurance; in other words,
   it will bring your ego to its knees.

7. During a power test you will have the opportunity to call up every skill and resource you
   know to pass it. Part of the test is that you
   will doubt the effectiveness of what you
   know to do.

Initiations into the inner forms of power seldom
occur in a public or social arena. They are usually deep
personal recognitions resulting from difficult inner
and outer tests and challenges. Often there is no visible
indication that such an initiation has been passed
through, nor can these initiations be advertised or, like
credentials, be placed behind your name. The proof you
have passed a challenge is in your ability to take on new
responsibilities and handle power more effectively. The
key to the fact that you have been initiated is that recognizable power comes to you.

Our friend and colleague Brian Arthur, an internationally recognized economist, felt a strong inner push
to write a book outlining his latest thinking on the
changing economic structures and the new economy

created by the rapid proliferation of high technology. Before he could write, he felt a voice inside tell him that he must spend time in the wilderness and go within for a time. In this manner he could realize the writing of his book.

Without hesitation, he cancelled important meetings and obligations and headed for Baja, California, where he underwent a two-week solo stay on the desolate coastline there. He spent the time fasting, contemplating, watching the surf, observing the birds, feeling the wind, and observing his own inner states. He experienced extensive periods of boredom during his sojourn on the cliffs overlooking the Pacific. For long periods of time he experienced nothing, no profound thoughts, no insights, no epiphanies. He endured flies, windblown sand, heat, a badly twisted ankle, and moments when he wondered why he was there. On the final day, sunburned, windburned, and thinner, he packed up and headed for his car; and he didn't feel that he had discovered anything particularly new for his book.

When he returned to the States, he sat down at his computer, and the ideas flooded out. He was so energized, he wrote night and day and could hardly keep up with the flow of ideas.

There are several important keys to understanding this powerful initiatory experience:

1. Brian listened to an inner voice telling him to do something that was very inconvenient;

it was costly in terms of time and lost income, and certainly uncomfortable physically and emotionally.

2. He did not have the benefit of any corporation or group of people sanctioning his wilderness experience.

3. He brought back no visible rewards, no certificate, credential, or promotion to show for his efforts.

4. He had few people he could tell about his experience who would understand it.

5. He had no way of knowing ahead of time if his efforts would prove fruitful.

6. He undertook the journey and remained, despite sacrificing income, inconveniencing himself and others, enduring physical discomfort, tolerating mental chatter, and suffering boredom.

7. He did not experience a breakthrough during his time on the desert coast. Only afterward did he enjoy the massive outpouring of insight and clarity.

Four Qualities for Success in a Test of Power

You will need four qualities if you are to set up conditions for successfully negotiating a power test or initiation. Although they will manifest differently, these qualities are the same whether the initiation is for inner power or external power. They are *commitment, sacrifice, perseverance,* and *faith.*

Commitment accompanied your decision to make a power bid in the first place. Your goal, the end result you hope for, is a reflection of your commitment. Understanding why you are going through the initiation by keeping track of what you hope to achieve will keep you on the path.

José could have given up the dream of getting a doctorate after failing the exam the first or second time, but his commitment to certain work in the world required him to have this credential. Brian, the economist, was committed to his goal of writing a book.

The quality of sacrifice is one people who are addicted to comfort and instant gratification do not understand or have much experience with. What you sacrifice during a power test is your current level of comfort, your preconceived ideas, and attitudes. If you are expanding your business, all your files and ways of doing things may be in chaos for a time — yet this is a sacrifice with potentially great rewards. The test and initiation in this case might be that you lose many of your employees whose comfort level has been threatened, or you may come up against public criticism from your competitors, or you may have unexpected difficulty obtaining the business loan you need. In José's case, the sacrifice included both time and ego. In Brian's case, the sacrifice included risking judgment from friends and colleagues and intense physical discomfort.

Sacrifice during a test of power will also typically include even renouncing for a time the ability to see oneself as competent, knowledgeable, productive, and successful.

Perseverance is the quality that keeps you going during an initiation. It keeps you from giving up, keeps you trying again and again, learning from your mistakes. If toddlers gave up learning to walk after the first few tries at taking a few steps, no one would ever walk. Mountain climbers all have firsthand experience with this quality, as their very lives often depend on their ability to persevere. Anyone who has ever climbed a mountain and made it to the top will certainly agree that this is a valid initiation that leads to greater power.

Finally, faith is essential. No initiation or test can be successfully negotiated without a great deal of faith. Faith is the quality that keeps one persevering even when nothing seems to make sense anymore. Faith also allows for the right timing of the final break-through in initiation for inner power and in the successful end result of an initiation for visible, external power. Brian Arthur had faith that the solitary time he spent would be fruitful and lead to visible productivity and insights even though he experienced neither during his stay. José, although enduring temporary moments of despair, had faith that all the hard work, study, sacrifice, and perseverance would lead ultimately to a doctorate.

If you have faith, you need not always know all the steps in the power test that will lead to success. You can more easily trust that what you cannot see or understand will still lead you through your initiation successfully, provided that you have entered into it as a bid for more power with all the right ingredients.

Exercise: Bidding for Power

Consider some of the bids for power you have undertaken in your life. What was the price for those bids? What kind of discomfort did you endure? What initiations did you go through and what was the process like? Were there outer initiations or deep internal ones?

What have you committed to with regard to your work? What are the sacrifices you have made to get where you are now? Were the sacrifices too high for your ambitions? Were they worth it? What helped you to persevere through the hard times? What supported your faith in yourself that you would prevail?

SUMMARY

Important Concepts to Remember:

- According to shamanic tradition, bidding for power, whether at the visible or invisible level, always comes with a price.
- The price of power will be your own comfort level.
- A successful bid for power is always acknowledged by an initiation.

- Initiations at both the inner and outer levels
  mark increasing levels of power.
- The four qualities needed for successfully
  negotiating a test or initiation are

1. Commitment.
2. Sacrifice.
3. Perseverance.
4. Faith.

Part 2

BALANCING POWER

Chapter 10

THE FIVE SHAMANIC VALUES

To associate not with the foolish,
To be with the wise,
To honor the worthy ones,
This is the blessing supreme.

— Buddha

Make the company you keep keep the company strong.

— Harvey Mackay, *Pushing the Envelope*

RULE 3 CONTINUED

Power in itself is neutral. It is neither good nor bad.
It just is. How you manage it determines the
positive or negative consequences for you and others.

In keeping with our rule, shamans exercise power
in a great many ways. Some use it compassionately and

productively while others use power for negative purposes. The power itself is neutral and as shamans move
through stages of personal development, they learn to
wield it without attachment.

What is true of shamans is true of anyone. It would
be naive to assume that every shaman is a great master,
a wise teacher, or an exceptional person. Shamans come
from the great pool of humanity, and therefore we find
every aspect of human nature in this select group of
people. Like everyone else, shamans come with different skills, talents, value systems, and motives, and they
exist in different states of evolution vis-à-vis their own
calling.

Shamans differentiate among themselves who is an
apprentice, who has average skills, who is good at what
they do, and who is a true master. By looking at the different categories of shamanic expertise, we can begin
to understand the categories that distinguish businesspeople as well, because they are the same.

SKILLS

The first category relates to skill level. Obviously one
shaman will have more skills than another, regardless
of the number of years of experience. One shaman
may have rainmaking skills, excellence in storytelling,
the capability of remote viewing, and a powerful healing ability. Another may have the strong eye, a talent
for looking into the future, an excellence with performing ceremonies, and a powerful sense of humor.

EXPERIENCE

In the area of experience, one shaman may have fifty years of practice and another ten. As we all know, experience is not everything, but nonetheless it is very important. One shaman may have extensive experience with using medicinal plants while another is still apprenticing in this area.

TALENT

The third category is talent. One shaman may have great talent while another may have much less, regardless of the number of skills and years of experience. A young Peruvian shaman in his twenties is respected and highly admired by his colleagues, who are well into their sixties and seventies; they even go to him for advice on many matters.

VALUES

The fourth category, values, is the most important. Values have to do with what a shaman regards as meaningful and important; values determine what a shaman is willing and not willing to do with his or her powers, skills, and knowledge. Values are what motivate shamans to behave in certain ways regarding trust, service, sorcery, healing, influence, and so on. Because it is the most important, it's good to focus on this fourth category and seek to understand the different value systems of shamans. Once we do this, we can see parallels with the values of people in business. We have found that understanding these sets of values is a key to understanding power.

There are five sets of values that influence the behavior of shamans. Because anthropologists have failed to differentiate these value systems, they have likewise failed to understand a great deal about shamans and their activities. They have either overly romanticized them or utterly dismissed them as simply primitive people. Neither extreme view is accurate. The truth is that shamans are like everyone else, some mediocre, some great. We want to know what makes a master shaman because then we will know what makes a great business or organizational leader.

These five sets of values step up the ladder of a shaman's evolution, moving to higher levels of sophistication, knowledge, and power.

Survival Oriented

The first and most primitive value system is the survival-oriented shaman. Shamans that are primarily survival oriented tend to be highly superstitious, deeply afraid, and willing to do anything to survive. This can even include murdering opponents, planting curses, and engaging in black magic to harm people and promote their own selfish agendas. They are absolutely ruthless, cannot be reasoned with, and do not understand the concepts of service, love, interrelatedness, and selflessness. Anyone who wants to have a peaceful and happy life should consider them very dangerous and avoid them. They have a type of power but are not truly powerful.

It's possible to find similar types in the business world: psychopaths, utterly ruthless con artists, people who deal with harmful substances, and individuals who will bribe, bait and switch, and resort to dirty tricks to carry out their business plans. They create conflict and discord, and inevitably lose their power.

Rule Oriented

The next step up in development from survival-oriented shaman is the rule-oriented shaman. This is similar to the evolution of an infant to a toddler. Rule-oriented shamans tend to be rigid, orthodox, and inflexible. They do not deviate from what they have been taught; they do everything according to an exact, established set of rituals. They are not psychologically sophisticated or insightful and tend to blame problems on external forces. A headache is always a curse sent by an opposing shaman. A lost object or misfortune is always caused by an unfriendly relative or a business opponent. This way of thinking causes them to justify harming others and perceiving of others as enemies. These shamans are frequently engaged in warfare with other shamans because they are attached to limited belief systems that place them in opposition to other sets of rules and traditions.

The business world is filled with small-minded

bureaucrats, inflexible in their thinking, attached to traditional but outmoded methods, protective of their turf, and inclined to blame all problems on external forces. They attempt to maintain the status quo even as great changes are happening all around them. They do not fare well with the forces of change, they try to hang onto their security, and they resist what they do not understand. The result, of course, is a loss of power.

Success Oriented

After the toddler rigidity of the rule-oriented shaman comes the next level of development, success orientation, akin to the interests of a latency-age child. Success-oriented shamans tend to focus primarily on reputation. What is meaningful and important to them is being known, having the most powerful influence, and being highly successful, regardless of the means. They are often adept at psychological warfare, at taking advantage of others' weaknesses, and are politically sophisticated, promoting themselves shamelessly for their own success. They want to win at all costs, and they will gladly sacrifice others on the altar of their own drive for achievement. For a success-oriented shaman, appearance is everything. In the Philippines there are some psychic surgeons with powerful reputations and great personal wealth who regularly use slight-of-hand to deceive their patients into believing tumors and cancers have been removed. Not all psychic surgeons perform in this manner, but there are many who do.

Success-oriented shamans are focused primarily on

visible power, and they are often quite good at manipulating physical forces to get what they want.

Success orientation in business is certainly a vital part of the game, and all players must have some degree of this motivation to play the game at all. There is a difference, however, between a person whose primary motivator is to win at all costs and someone who places a priority on winning but an even higher priority on quality and service.

The value system of the former type motivates a leader to pile on the work and increase the time load on an ever shrinking pool of workers in the name of a greater profit margin. The shortsightedness of this approach reveals itself in an exhausted, demoralized workforce that lives in fear of not looking busy enough. This business type stops at nothing to win the game, even if the outcome robs the public of the best quality or most advanced products. Recent revelations in the computer industry clearly point to this philosophy as a primary motivator in a major player. From our point of view, this kind of power play will always exact the high price of a loss of power.

Relationship Oriented

The next step up the ladder of a shaman's evolution is to become motivated primarily by a desire to be of service to others. Here the child has grown to young adulthood. The shaman is now more relationship oriented, and success at all costs gives way to a desire to heal and be helpful to others. At this level of sophistication, a shaman is willing to forgo fees, donate time, and go out of the way to help those less fortunate. What these shamans lose in time and fees to those in difficulty they easily make up from those who have means. This shift in values represents a major power increase because at this higher level of understanding, a shaman can operate from a position where differences and separation between people fall away — and the less separation, the greater the power of the shaman to heal.

Relationship-oriented shamans tend to have solid relationships among themselves as well as others, and this allows them to go deep within to access power and knowledge denied to externally oriented shamans who pursue visible power through intimidation and manipulation. The energy that is tied up in this self-oriented behavior becomes free for use in service to the world at large.

Relationship-oriented shamans display deep psychological insights into others. They operate from a position of flexibility and will do whatever it takes to assist others with their difficulties. They do not necessarily look to tradition to tell them what to do, rather they go with their own inner authority. One disadvantage of this orientation is that it can sometimes lead these shamans to neglect their own well-being and work themselves to exhaustion.

The relationship-oriented person in business is a new breed of manager. Increasingly, the business world is seeing the influence of this value orientation from people who seek to shift management from a vertical to a more horizontal style. They value the worker and sense that long-term profits are far greater with policies that lead to employee satisfaction and morale rather than to policies that bring about near virtual slavery. Relationship-oriented business leaders care about employees, work side by side with them, and place a high priority on high-quality communication. The result of course is an increase in power for everyone involved.

Philosophically Oriented

The philosophically oriented shamans are the master shamans, the truly great leaders who stand out head and shoulders among their peers. The young adult has now grown into the wise elder. They have achieved such an abundance of personal power that they don't need to expend any energy on either self-defense or self-promotion. They create no heroes, do not seek approval from other authorities, and can discover answers simply by looking deeply within for confirmation of what they suspect is true.

Philosophically oriented shamans are powerfully intuitive, able to see with the strong eye right through others as if they were transparent. They tend to be direct, ruthlessly honest, but at the same time deeply compassionate and loving. They are no one's fool and command respect even from those who disagree with them or even oppose them. They are attached to no protocol, set ways, or rituals but are always spontaneous and flexible, constantly surprising people with their unpredictable but brilliant solutions to problems. They are detached from appearances and outward signs of success; they are completely dedicated to the pursuit of truth. They have awakened from the mass hypnosis, the trancelike amnesia that most people are lost in. Their priority is impeccability in thought, word, and deed. They realize that they are completely responsible for what they say and how they say it, and that blaming others for anything is pure folly.

Their intent and attention are so well developed that they can suspend ordinary physical laws to influence the outcome of events. Many of them can even communicate with the elements to the degree that they alter weather patterns for the sake of the well-being of people.

Philosophically oriented master shamans are aware of this important truth: To achieve a desired end, they must let go of their attachment to the outcome. They are not powerful because they want power; they are powerful because they are not attached to their own power and are willing to relinquish it if that is what they perceive as the right action.

This type of master shaman always seems to have a raucous sense of humor and often is incredibly irreverent. They simply do not care what other people think and this gives them effectiveness and wisdom beyond measure. They are disciplined yet relaxed, dominant yet submissive, strong yet humble. They are deadly serious yet have a twinkle in their eye; they are nondescript yet unforgettable.

Philosophically oriented business leaders are, in

many ways, no different in values from master shamans; they are in reality masters themselves, simply in a different costume. They have a strong focus on the truth; they are powerfully attentive and disciplined yet appear calm and relaxed, even easy going. They are not attached to convention and are always willing to take risks and abandon old systems and methods for new ones.

Philosophically oriented business leaders have natural authority and command attention and respect even if what they say seems to defy convention or rationality. They are not afraid to be alone, to meditate, to reflect, and to take swift action in the name of their inner authority. They have access to true power and are the finest role models for us to emulate.

SUMMARY

Important Concepts to Remember

- Power in itself is neutral. It is neither good nor bad.
- What you do with power determines the positive or negative consequences for you and others.
- By looking at the different categories of shamanic expertise, we can also begin to understand the categories that distinguish businesspeople from one another as well.
- We can place different categories into an order of significance, with the most important being

last: (1) skills; (2) experience; (3) talent; and
(4) values.

- Values determine what shamans choose to do
  with their powers, skills, and knowledge;
  values determine what a shaman is willing
  and not willing to do with his or her power,
  skills, and knowledge.
- Five sets of values step up the ladder of a
  shaman's evolution, moving to higher levels
  of sophistication, knowledge, and power.

1. Survival oriented.

2. Rule oriented.

3. Success oriented.

4. Relationship oriented.

5. Philosophically oriented.

These same five sets of values are found in
the business community as well.

Chapter 11

THE SEVEN EXPRESSIONS OF POWER

According to Mongolian shamanism, the ideal way to live is best described by the word *tegsh,* which means "being in balance" and which implies acting in moderation but also with consideration for the effects of one's actions upon others.

— Sarangerel, Mongolian shaman, *Riding Windhorses: A Journey into the Heart of Mongolian Shamanism*

RULE 7

Power must be ridden as a surfer rides a wave: balance is everything on the power path.

THE DIFFERENT
EXPRESSIONS OF POWER

Power does not express itself through only one modality. Shamans who have gained true wisdom have long known this and emphasize developing different parts of themselves in their long training and in the training of their apprentices. They say that power comes in seven different forms. Although individuals will display more or less talent in the different areas, each form must be developed to help them form a greater balance of skills and abilities.

The seven forms of power are:

1. Artist
2. Storyteller
3. Warrior
4. Chief
5. Priest
6. Healer
7. Teacher

These seven modes of expression of shamanic power likewise describe the ideal business or organizational leader, who is part artist, storyteller, warrior, chief, priest, healer, and teacher.

Artist

Artists are visionaries, able to see ahead, to penetrate the future and portray it in the present in artistic form through sign and symbol. From the tattoos of the Maori in New Zealand and the aboriginals in New Guinea to the body painting of the Australian aborigines, from the totem carvings of the Inuit to the rock art of the Native American, from the cave art at Lascaux to the drum paintings of the Sammi in Finland, shamanic art is evident on all continents of the world.

Tibetan and Navajo shamans are famous for their elaborate paintings of colored sand, unique creations that require many days of painstaking work, only to be instantaneously obliterated at the chosen moment. The Huichols of Mexico portray their peyote visions and ceremonies in exquisite yarn art that is fast becoming world famous. From beadwork to carving, feather work to sculpture, shamans the world over engage their creative expression in sacred art.

For shamans, all of life is the flow of creativity through intense personal expression, applied imagination; life is art in motion. A shaman knows that the world is a canvas on which anything can be painted. Through artistic expression, shamans harness the creative energies of nature: plants, animals, minerals, wind, water, and fire. They understand that these elements are channels or vehicles of a single creative energy whose source is in the spirit world. Shamans have learned through discipline to focus their creativity with powerful intent, and this intention helps to form events in the physical world. Thus the carving of a wooden fish done with gratitude and conscious intent can make for an excellent catch.

This same knowledge of conscious intent leads to expression through dance and the music of instrument and voice. Just as cross-culturally there are similar patterns in the examples of shamanic art, so there are universal themes in the dances and songs of shamans all over the world. These themes reflect gratitude for the help of the spirit world, intent for a prosperous endeavor in planting or hunting, or the desire to heal a difficulty or disease. In addition, shamanic songs and dances are records of the dangers and benefits of interacting with the spirit world.

A master organizational leader is likewise a visionary, able to look into the future to sense the next trends before anyone else identifies them. Master business leaders are people with a special appreciation for beauty and self-expression. Every successful visionary business leader we know has an excellent eye for art, an appreciation for music and good food. These artistic leanings are not accidental and are associated with the artist-visionary qualities master shamans choose to cultivate.

Storyteller

The world of shamanism is a world of myth and metaphor. In all parts of the planet, shamans share common creation myths that describe a paradise lost, a series of catastrophic geological events that separated humans from the great light in the sky. Similarly, shamanic myths tell of a great tree soaring into the sky with roots around the earth that divides the universe into the lower, middle, and upper worlds, each in turn divided into the four cardinal directions. These myths, handed down orally through countless generations, are a kind of shamanic history of consciousness, and its preservation relies on the storytelling powers of the shaman, dramatist, orator, and actor.

Shamans rely on drama as a key to the impact of the myth on their listeners. They act out their story with dance, song, and colorful expression. The earliest form of theater was shamanic, a method of teaching and sharing with everyone a powerful mystical experience. Shamans must, then, cultivate the skill of public speaking, develop the powers to inspire and move members of their communities, and practice the art of persuasion: good shamans are master salespeople.

Of course, the master business leader, the mover and shaker who must inspire people to take risks and meet ever greater challenges, exhibit these very traits. Powerful business leaders speak in metaphor, tell stories about their vision, influence, persuade, and sell their visions. The better their public speaking abilities, the more power they acquire and manifest.

Warrior

Shamanism is reflective and contemplative and yet action oriented as well. Shamans spend time in solitude and meditation, but when challenged by internal or external obstacles and dangers, they also must develop the warrior within, armed with the weapons of concentration and courage, discipline and intent, impeccability and trustworthiness. A shaman needs strength to endure the rigors of vision questing, fasting, and demanding ceremonies that may require nights and days of chanting and drumming. The shaman battles with disease, spirit loss, and negativity on behalf of the person who comes for healing. The shaman fights fatigue, distraction, and laziness in the constant quest for power.

Shamans are historically famous for battling demons and malevolent spirits. They can protect their people from negative spirits, natural disasters, and human as well as animal enemies. The shaman who demonstrates the greatest power enjoys the greatest trust from the community.

One of the greatest examples of the warrior-shaman was Geronimo, the Apache chief who managed to mystically elude the United States Army for years before he gave himself up of his own accord. Geronimo gained the highest respect and even awe from his enemies because of his complete dedication to protecting his people, for his bravery, discipline, and unusual shamanic skills that helped him to vanish with his braves at moments of almost certain defeat. Even today Geronimo holds a powerful reputation as the type of warrior not to fight with.

Great business leaders are also good warriors. They fight for their employees. They fight attempts to destroy the community they have worked so hard to create. They fight demoralizing influences, which are akin to the spirit loss a shaman must fight against.

They fight business demons; they battle to heal the deep wounds and divisions that arise in their corporations.

A great business leader must develop the traits that a warrior-shaman cultivates: concentration, courage, discipline, intent, impeccability, and trustworthiness.

Chief

Shamans work to develop their personal powers, and with their success comes leadership. The more powerful a shaman becomes, the more natural authority that shaman has in the community. Shamanic power comes from garnering plant and animal allies, and also from personal mastery.

Shamans often prove to be adept leaders in trade and commerce. They are commonly the most prosperous members of their communities. Powerful shamans manage to magnetically attract whatever they need for personal and tribal survival, and they frequently provide for the less prosperous members of the community, distributing their wealth as they see fit.

With their ability to protect and provide for those around them, shamans have always been the pillars of their communities. In ancient times emperors, kings, and monarchs were expected to be shamans as well, individuals who had mastered themselves and developed powers to protect their realms from enemies and to bring prosperity to their people. The story of King Arthur is one example of the mystical shaman-king.

The most masterful business leaders exhibit all the

powers of the shaman-chief, leaders whom the people respect and listen to for their sage wisdom and direction. Leaders who have this kind of power are invariably good listeners, great role models, and successful at attracting wealth and prosperity to their organizations.

Priest

Shamans are the priests and ministers of their communities — though this does not mean that they necessarily have authority over anyone. They act as intermediaries between the spirit world and ordinary reality. People believe them capable of communicating with the dead; they conduct ceremonies to honor ancestors or release them from being earthbound. They can enter the world of non-ordinary reality at will through the symbolic entrances to the spirit world. They use ordinary materials such as smoke, rattles, and drums to transport their consciousness to wherever they wish to go in the physical or spirit worlds.

They are highly respected and are natural counselors for their communities.

Although the business world is mostly a secular one and carries in it deep suspicions of anything even suggesting the supernatural, a great business leader nonetheless will find that people often turn to them for things of the spirit — inspiration, vision, understanding, and even some attention to ceremony. We have known business leaders who understood this to be an important part of their work and never missed an opportunity to create a ceremony around launching a new project or service, giving an inspirational sermon to raise morale, or stopping to give counsel to an employee who needed a little extra help.

Healer

Shamanism is a tradition of healing and curing. Since the dawn of time, shamans have been the doctors, the healing members of their tribes through their knowledge of herbs, ceremony, prayers, and journeys into the spirit realm. They treat and heal all manner of conditions, from emotional imbalances to cancerous growths and blindness. Their knowledge and power have sustained the trust and faith of the people who rely on them since ancient times.

Shamans are the original psychotherapists and marriage counselors. Their deep understanding of character and personality and their keen awareness of the impact of their words bring the members of their communities to them for therapy and counsel. They are often called upon to mediate conflicts and resolve disputes. Their own willingness to undergo hardship and sacrifice for their communities inspires others as well.

A masterful business leader, too, is a good psychologist, a nurturer, healer of people and organizations as well. Members of the business community and entire organizations striving to fulfill their missions can take a terrible beating from competition, changing laws, and fluctuating conditions. Wounds can run deep and blood can symbolically flow — emotionally and financially. A powerful leader will know how to heal wounds, raise spirits, and find solutions in dire situations. Business leaders who are healers understand how to diagnose the real problem and address it effectively.

Teacher

The teacher-shaman is a seeker of knowledge, one who pursues truth wherever it might be found. Knowing the great power of knowledge and the great risks that we take when we lack knowledge shamans invest much time and effort in gaining it. Whether they are forecasting the weather or predicting personal fortune, they enter a world where others fear to tread. Not only is their task difficult but they also risk the loss of reputation and trust — even death in some cases — if they turn out to be wrong. For the advanced shaman, knowledge is a great power and is never to be taken for granted.

Teacher-shamans are also eager students, keen to learn from their experience and from their observations of all that surrounds them — the elements, the worlds of plants and animals, other shamans, and members of their communities. A master teacher is always a good student, willing to learn and willing to apply their learning to action. They find resources everywhere and are grateful to the sources of their information.

A good business leader must also be a person of knowledge, a good teacher, and an eager student, always learning from their mistakes and the mistakes of others as well. Like a good shaman, they do not confuse information with knowledge, understanding that information by itself is useless, whereas knowledge —

knowing how to put information to good use — is supremely valuable.

All forms of power within the shamanic tradition can be discovered within the context of this seven-sided world-view. Although many of these forms of power overlap, each reflects a unique quality of shamanism that is essential for success. When we see the power that results from the development of the seven aspects of a master shaman, we can understand why shamanism has survived the great twin tests of time and cultural change, and why it continues to survive even with the presence of modern science and business practice, even with the historical efforts of foreign religions to stamp it out.

Shamanism can coexist with modern science, business, and religion because its context is so vast that it encompasses all phenomena. Shamanism is a balanced human perspective and practice that returns power to the individual. Most important, shamanism is a set of strategies available to anyone with an interest in discovering them and is especially useful for people in the business world and the world of organizations.

SUMMARY

Important Concepts to Remember

- Power comes in seven different forms or expressions. The seven shamanic forms of power are:

1. Artist
2. Storyteller
3. Warrior
4. Chief
5. Priest
6. Healer
7. Teacher

- Although individuals will display more or less talent in the different areas, each form must be developed.
- Master business leaders demonstrate aspects of these seven forms of power as well.

Chapter 12

DOING AND BEING

The questions that heal us and offer hope for authentic change are the ones we cannot easily answer. Living systems are not controllable, despite the fact that they evolve toward order and some cohesion. To move a living system, we need to question what we are doing and why. We need to choose depth over speed, consciousness over action. At least for a little while.

— Peter Block, *Flawless Consulting:*
A Guide to Getting Your Expertise Used

Shamanism is both an epistemology, that is a system of contemplative thought with an implicit set of propositions, and a blueprint for action, as in the location of game animals or the retrieval of kidnapped souls.

— Jeremy Narby and Francis Huxley, *Shamans through Time: Five*
Hundred Years on the Path to Knowledge

RULE 7 CONTINUED

Power must be ridden as a surfer rides a wave: balance is everything on the power path.

We have learned that power is not something that you can ever own or accumulate on a permanent basis. A shaman would say that power can be accumulated and conserved, but it can also be dissipated without proper care or attention. Think of power as something like electricity that can be accessed in different wattages. When you become more powerful, it is not that you own that power but rather that you learn to access and handle stronger wattages of it when necessary. You can learn to plug into more power and use it without burning yourself out. Some people can use only very small amounts of power and some have developed and earned the ability to use very large amounts of it.

As with electricity, you must always handle power with great care or risk hurting yourself and others. An experienced shaman knows that you can never grow careless around power or you may pay severe consequences. Novices tend to forget this and create difficult situations for themselves and others by forgetting to pay attention to this important principle. Many politicians forget to handle power with care as well: To a shaman they are like children playing with fire, with no idea of the harm they do to themselves and others with its abuse.

Power, then, is like a standing wave, always ready to take you for a ride. Riding it successfully requires knowledge of its turbulence, its quirks and unpredictability, like the surfer who learns with experience to handle large, even potentially deadly waves with grace and aplomb. The key to both surfing a wave and handling power is *balance*. Without it you will surely fall.

To find this balance, we need to develop harmony within our own psyches in a variety of ways. First, it means learning to balance the masculine side of ourselves with the feminine side. Without this balance, we will lean too heavily to one side or the other, tipping over into difficulties in many areas of our lives. The result of losing your balance may very well include the following difficulties:

Imbalance toward the Male Side, or Too Much Sun

- Inability to listen
- Inability to communicate well with women
- Heavy-handedness in leadership roles
- "Analysis paralysis," or allowing the intellect to dominate obsessively
- Overreliance on deductive reasoning
- Obsession with details
- Addiction to impulsive action
- Impatience
- Depression and a tendency to hold onto grief
- Stubbornness
- Arrogance
- Greed
- Autocratic decision making
- Desire to control others

Imbalance toward the Female Side, or Too Much Moon

- Inability to speak up
- Inability to communicate well with men
- Passiveness in leadership roles
- Emotionalism, or difficulty in being objective
- Overanxiety in making decisions
- Tendency toward vagueness
- Hypercriticism of yourself and others
- Self-deprecation
- Passive-aggressiveness
- Martyr or victim role
- Desire for others to make decisions and take responsibility
- Overanxiety to please
- Out-of-control feeling

Exercise: Sun or Moon

Look over the lists above and check the traits that apply to you. You may have checks in both lists, indicating that you fall off either side of the surfboard. You will probably have far more checks in one list than the other, however, suggesting you regularly fall off only one side of the board.

To find balance you will need to move toward the positive qualities of the side of you that you have most neglected. If you tend to be overly vague and anxious over decision making, then you need to develop more confidence and regularly practice decision making. If you tend to act impulsively without taking stock of a situation and tend to be controlling, then you need to become more aware of the needs of others, and learn to delegate more and micromanage less.

Balancing Doing with Being

The second thing you must learn to become balanced is how to match doing with being, something that the business world knows very little about. Consider that *to be* is a verb, an action word. To be means to live, exist, endure, and persist. Shamans know that being is vitally important in their pursuit of power. They know that doing with too little emphasis on being tends to lead to a great many mistakes. To do things well requires reflection, meditation, contemplation, and quieting the mind.

During the Vietnam War, General Westmoreland's policy was to attack the North Vietnamese with heavy forces, tanks, mortars, and air power and raze the landscape in a great display of doing. The North Vietnamese would simply disappear, only to reappear in a couple of days totally unscathed. This is a classic lesson about the inadequacy of overdoing and neglecting, in this example, to closely observe the enemy's strategy. Being is observing. You must watch, look, and listen carefully, go deep inside, and then strike like lightning. This is how a tiny nation defeated a behemoth.

The key to doing well, then, is not to be constantly doing. The whole idea of constantly doing comes from the puritanical notion that "idle hands are the devil's

workshop." This can translate to employees endlessly
trying to look busy for fear they will seem idle when the
supervisor walks by. The shamanic approach says that
this pretense of constantly doing is absurd just as over-
working is out of balance. Doing is only effective when
it follows a period of contemplation. Then the key is to
strike like a cougar attacking its prey. A cougar that spent
all its time trying to look busy would be completely ineffective as a predator. The experienced shaman understands that knowledge comes from observing the natural
landscape; the shaman says, "Watch the cougar. See how
the cougar waits and studies its prey. Be, then do." A
carefully constructed balance of being and doing is the
secret of success. Notice that balance does not mean
equal parts of each: Observing usually takes much longer
than action; the action often takes only a few moments.

On the other hand, mostly being, with little or no
doing, may be effective for spiritual development but
can be highly unproductive in the work world. We don't
need to do more than mention this side of the equation,
however, because this is not the average businessperson's problem, particularly in the highly industrial-
ized societies.

Exercise: Doing and Being

Observe yourself throughout the course of a typical
workday. Keep a notepad handy and track the various
times of doing and being throughout your day. How
much time do you actually spend being? Reading your
e-mail is not being. Reading the newspaper is not

being. Walking briskly to a meeting is not being. What is being? Being is attending, contemplating, dreaming, absorbing, considering, watching, noticing, looking within, grasping, and intuiting. Being is watching your breath, feeling the energy or presence within your body, and meditating. If you have trouble understanding what these states are, then you need more being in your life.

Awareness of Spirit

The third thing you need to develop to be balanced is an awareness of your dual dimensionality — both the physical body, with the outer personality associated with your everyday doing, and your inner, less visible dimension, which shamans sometimes call the spirit body. Most people are either completely unaware or only vaguely aware of this second, more essential dimension that is profoundly associated with true power. This is so vitally important to the shamanic way and to the acquisition of power that we have devoted the following chapter to it. Developing these two dimensions is vital to achieving balance.

SUMMARY

Important Concepts to Remember

- Power can be ridden as a surfer rides a wave.
- Balance is everything on the power path.
- To find balance, we need to develop harmony

by learning to balance the masculine and feminine sides of ourselves.

- Doing, with too little emphasis on being, tends to lead to a great many mistakes.
- To do things well requires reflection, meditation, contemplation, and quieting the mind.
- To truly become balanced and powerful requires an awareness of spirit.

Chapter 13

THE TWO STATES OF ATTENTION

An individual's inner consciousness is always accessible. In practice, most of us are seldom in communication with it, because we are so rarely encouraged to look within for guidance or answers. As a result, we tend to compromise our ability to perform and our willingness to assume total responsibility for our work environments.

— William A. Guillory, *The Living Organization —
Spirituality in the Workplace*

There are a variety of ways to open up to the second field. In general, doing so demands stepping beyond ordinary conditional fields.

— Ken Eagle Feather, *A Toltec Path*

RULE 7 CONTINUED

Power must be ridden as a surfer rides a wave: balance is everything on the power path.

THE TWO ATTENTIONS

Shamans the world over identify two distinct states of attention that must be clearly understood and learned to acquire real power. Shamans of the Toltec tradition in North and Central America use the term "first attention" to describe how the majority of people see physical reality most of the time. The first attention is what we use to identify everyday objects and perceive the ordinary world. In the first attention a cave is a hole in the ground, a chair is something to sit on, a tree is for shade or lumber, and so on. The first attention is so constantly used that most people cannot imagine any other way of perceiving.

There is, however, another level of perception into an entirely different set of realities that Toltec shamans call the "second attention." Michael Harner, the American anthropologist who has spent a career studying shamanism, calls this set of realities "non-ordinary reality." This reality can be seen with the second attention. The second attention is a term used to describe a vast number of states and realities that shamans and visionaries all over the world access through questing, prayer, meditation, dance, and countless other means. To someone using the second attention, a cave might be a doorway into hidden realities of the spirit world where solutions to problems exist, a chair might be holding a past occupant's thoughts and feelings and therefore might be harmful to sit in, a tree might be an ally, a powerful helping spirit.

Primacy of the First Attention

Since most people are aware of only the first attention, they tend to deny the existence of the second, claiming that it is simply superstition, illusion, or imagination. A shaman might respond to this dismissal, however, with this question: "What is not imagination?" Such an insight is difficult to grasp for people who use only the first attention, and if they even begin to understand it, it challenges their deep beliefs about the nature of reality — and that can be confusing and frightening. The safest thing to do is to change the subject. It takes courage to keep the dialogue open. But if you persist, you will open the door to the second attention and eventually learn through first-hand experience what is based in truth and what is actually an illusion.

According to the shamanic perspective, the first state of attention is so mesmerizing and trance inducing that most people are held fast in its confines. It is similar to being in a prison or in a bad dream. While at times the first attention can bring pleasure and even beauty, it has no real power because it is actually just a phantom, like the image in a mirror, only seeming to have substance but in fact being simply a reflection. As physicists discovered in the past century, what we call concrete reality is in fact empty space; the solidity of all objects is a figment of our imagination. Our ordinary reality, in other words, doesn't really exist.

The Two Attentions and Business

In the world of business, too, you can choose to see through the eyes of the first attention or through the eyes of the second. If you choose to see through only the first attention, then you might be able to move money, resources, and people around like pawns on a chessboard, but you can accomplish little because you're working on a superficial level. It is like trying to make things happen by altering your reflection in the mirror rather than altering yourself. If you saw someone trying to do this you would probably laugh and shake your head and think them ignorant, naive, or crazy. This is exactly what shamans think when they see the average modern businessperson trying to get things done by endless superficial maneuvering.

Qualities of the Second Attention

Shamans and many indigenous peoples find true power in the second attention, a realm that is difficult to describe, especially to people of the modern world. The second attention is a way of seeing, a ground of being. This state is needed to perceive what indigenous peoples call the spirit world, the *nagual*, the background to everything that is invisible to the first attention.

You must understand that everything seen through the first attention, the physical objects of the ordinary world, are contained in the world of the second attention, the spirit world. So, if you see with only the first attention, you see only a small piece of reality. If you see with the second attention, however, you see this small piece and gain access to the rest of reality as well. Obviously, for shamans interested in the survival and well-being of their people, developing access to the second attention is extremely important. Without it they would be as helpless and powerless as many modern businesspeople who, with every decision, create greater problems for themselves and others. If shamans used the same strategies that most people use to start a business, they would probably not survive longer than three years — just like most start-up businesses.

To better understand what the second attention actually makes perceivable, look at this list of some of its major qualities and try to apply them to your own experience:

- Experience of the second attention may occur in the bathroom, in a plane, an elevator, a church, your office, a meeting, or just about anywhere, anytime.
- To access it, you must be willing to let go — briefly — of the first attention. For many people this can be frightening.
- If you are unacquainted with the second attention, it may come upon you under extreme physical conditions. This is because it can only break through when the habitual dominance of the first attention is knocked out. It can occur spontaneously during a fever,

car accident, deprivation of food or drink,
extreme cold or heat, or another life-
threatening condition.

- The second attention need not be associated
  with suffering, however. It is available at any
  time by an act of intention. A master can
  induce it at will.

- The second attention uses your intellect but
  not your rationality.

- The second attention comes with strong, often
  unnamed feelings but not the ordinary kinds
  of emotion such as annoyance, desire, amuse-
  ment, or discouragement.

- You may experience the second attention in a
  state of either great stillness or extreme activity.

- You may induce the second attention by
  running, hypnosis, repetitive motions, danc-
  ing, listening to music, or being overwhelmed by nature. As an example,
  astronauts have frequently reported experiences of the second attention when seeing
  the earth from space.

- Ordinary experience of time and space is
  altered when second attention takes over.

- During the second attention, the usual
  notions of separation are broken down;
  boundaries dissolve.

- You may experience extremely fast motion as
  if traveling somewhere at a high rate of speed,
  even though your body is still. Or everything

might seem to move very slowly, at a snail's
pace.

- There may be a sense of déjà vu, a feeling that
the experience is completely familiar. You
might recognize an inner landscape as one
that you visit often in the dream state.

- You might recognize having forgotten something very important, only to be reminded of
it in this state.

- You may feel a profound sense of relief, joy,
or understanding.

- You may have sensations of spinning or
whirling at times.

- You may strongly feel the presence of a high
form of intelligence that is influencing you
or manifesting through you, but not controlling you.

- In deep states of second attention, dead rela-
tives, friends, or teachers may come into your
awareness who wish to communicate something important to you (like a warning not to
board a plane that later crashes).

- You might suddenly find the answer to a
dilemma presented to you in a flash of understanding.

- You might discover answers to problems that
other people have.

- You may experience seeing many dimensions
of something at once. For example, you may
see at the same time both the physical and

energetic aspects of a tree or plant. The energetic dimension of the plant may appear radically different from its physical state. The same
perception can occur of a person. A shaman
sees simultaneously the physical body and
other dimensions of a person, allowing the
shaman to perceive whether that person is
healthy, ill, or about to die.

• With practice, you can hold the second attention while using the first attention.

POWER AND THE
SECOND ATTENTION

This is only a partial list of the kinds of experiences available with the second attention. Since the second attention encompasses territory that is much more vast than
everyday reality, it is impossible to list everything about
it. With experience you can map the territory of the
second attention and even become good at maneuvering
through it, recognizing various landmarks, avoiding certain areas, and seeking out distinct locations.

Power, from the shamanic viewpoint, flows directly
from the world of spirit, the levels of reality that can be
perceived only through the second attention. If you want
to make something happen, don't restrict yourself to rear-
ranging the pawns in ordinary reality — you know this is
sure to fail. If you want to access real power, to walk the
power path, you must do it from the second attention.

A note of caution, however: You must pay close

attention to the first attention as well as the second or you will suffer from psychosis or a serious disorder in your ability to understand what is going on. You must master the qualities of the first attention as well as the second; then you become a walker between the worlds, a master of all, a slave of none. This is what shamans mean by balance.

Some businesspeople are well versed in the workings of the second attention, just as some professional athletes have discovered it under extreme performance conditions. They often hide the discovery, however, for fear of ridicule or misunderstanding. This is extremely unfortunate. The time has come for these profoundly powerful experiences to be seen as normal, helpful, and desirable.

According to the shamans of the world today, a natural occurrence in the evolution of the human race is allowing more and more people every day to perceive through the second attention. They say that eventually everyone will function using the second attention on a daily basis.

How to Apply the Second Attention to Business

1. Be willing to consider another way of perceiving beyond your ordinary everyday perspective.
2. Begin to cultivate the second attention by noticing the way it tries to break through to you, to get your attention in flashes of intuition and creative breakthroughs.

3. Set aside some time each day to cultivate the second attention; this can even be at work during a break or lunch, or during travel. Regularly setting time aside will increase the probability that you will have breakthroughs.

4. Pay more attention to your dreams; they are a window to the second attention. Write them down and spend more time considering their meaning.

5. Notice synchronicity more in your daily life. The surprise of seeing synchronicity can open the door to the second attention.

6. Instead of thinking in terms of *either/or,* think more in terms of *both/and.* Seeing the world in this way helps to open up the second attention.

7. Engage your body in rhythmical trance-inducing motions like running and drumming, or listen to trance-inducing music.

8. Break up your routine and do things in an entirely different order or simply do something you have never done before. This is good for opening up the second attention.

Exercises

Here are some useful shamanic techniques for cultivating the second attention. Some of them may seem unusual, different from what you are used to, but it is good to stretch your abilities, even though it may be a little uncomfortable at times.

Reflection: Stare at your reflection in a mirror and make direct eye contact for twenty minutes, or longer for a more powerful effect.

Shadows: Take a walk and focus only on the shadows of everything.

Soft focus: While walking outdoors, soften your focus; use all your senses to absorb everything around you — sounds, textures, colors, shapes, skin sensations, and thoughts — focusing on nothing specifically.

Background: Focus only on the background of the objects in your field of vision. Instead of seeing only the branches of a tree, focus more on the spaces between the branches of a tree, the space between the clouds, the space around a car, person, or building.

Male-Female: Using the power of your imagination, see the woman in every man and the man in every woman you interact with. Actually imagine them briefly as the opposite sex. Have fun with this — it can be an eye-opener. Become aware of male and female aspects as well — this can help us find balance and power.

SUMMARY

Important Concepts to Remember

- We use the first attention to perceive the ordinary world and identify everyday objects.
- The second attention is a way of seeing non-ordinary reality.

- Shamans and many indigenous peoples find true power in the second attention — for businesspeople as well, the source of true power is always found within the second attention.
- You must master the qualities of the first attention as well as the second; then you become a walker between the worlds, a master of all, a slave of none.
- We can access the second attention in even the most ordinary moment, including our daily schedule in our workplace and home life.
- According to shamans of the world today, a natural occurrence in the evolution of the human race is allowing more and more people every day to become aware of the second attention — the great key to power and further evolution.

Chapter 14

VISIBLE AND
INVISIBLE POWER

True leaders inspire people to do great things, and when the work is done, their people proudly say, "We did this ourselves."

— Lao-tzu

RULE 7 CONTINUED

Power must be ridden as a surfer rides a wave: balance is everything on the power path.

We have discussed how, for shamans, access to real power is through the second attention rather than the first. In the everyday business world, we typically define power as influence, control, force, might, and money, but we all know that these things are no guarantee of success in the world.

We have begun to explore a hidden power, a different kind of power that acts as a foundation of the more apparent and familiar types of power. These two very different types of power can be called visible power and invisible power. Both are important to know about and work with, and we must understand their relationship to one another as well. Learning to balance them is a key to success in business and in life.

For shamans, visible, external power depends on a foundation of invisible power. Using visible power alone will achieve only limited success, if any, and fail at the ultimate goal: winning the game of life, finding lasting happiness, fulfillment, and realizing your true life purpose. While you can, with great effort, manipulate visible power, appear powerful to others, and fool yourself — at least for a time — into thinking you are powerful, the shamanic perspective reveals that such power won't last. In the long run, visible power always fails to satisfy.

When visible power rests on the foundation of invisible power, then you can be truly powerful. This requires accumulating enough invisible power to get things to happen in the visible world.

Note that not everyone who has accumulated great invisible power chooses to manifest it externally. Sometimes those with a large store of invisible power are completely obscure individuals, not known to the public at large. They may serve their communities quietly and choose to live without attracting attention to themselves. When a person with great invisible power does choose to manifest it in the visible world, the impact is monumental. Jesus, Buddha, Gandhi, John Muir, St. Theresa, da Vinci, and Nikola Tesla are a few obvious examples.

Here are some examples to help illustrate the differences between visible and invisible power in the world of business. Remember that you can appear powerful for a time using only visible forms of power, but the power will be short-lived and easily overturned by one who uses both forms.

VISIBLE POWER

Visible power manifests in control, influencing external events, setting them in motion, ruling over others, and dominating in decision making. The following lists are limited and partial. As you read, try not to make judgments; simply take note.

Visible Power in Communication

A person displaying visible power in communication style is commonly the person who

- Introduces the topics
- Interrupts frequently

- Discloses no personal information but requires it of the other person
- Answers questions addressed to others
- Dominates conversation
- Dispenses with forms of courtesy and politeness while others feel bound to follow protocol
- Uses jargon or technical terms to exclude or condescend to listeners
- Demands others report to them
- Frequently passes judgment on others.

Visible Power in Behavior Patterns

In behavior patterns, the person tends to

- Summarily dismiss others
- Shake hands forcibly, or even with palm down to force the other into a subordinate position
- Make the other party wait for an audience or a reply to a query
- Keep a physical distance, often behind a barrier
- Be reserved emotionally and psychologically
- Assume the position of veteran while implying the other is a novice.

Visible Power in the Physical Situation

In terms of physical situation, the person will tend to

- Sit while the other person stands
- Place him- or herself in an elevated position with a large chair behind an imposing desk

- Face the entrance to a room while the other person has their back to it
- Take a seat at the head of a long table during meetings.

Symbols of Visible Power

Regarding displays of symbols of visible power, the person typically

- Adopts credentials, insignia, stripes, ornaments, or clothing indicative of rank
- Displays trophies, awards, acknowledgements, and testimonials
- Occupies an impressive corner office on an upper floor with an impressive view
- Has many assistants and aides
- Uses limousines and private jets.

INVISIBLE POWER

Invisible power is marked by alignment with the power inherent in a situation. It requires using the second attention to become aware of this subtle, radiant power. Using invisible power, you function in the moment from a strong, clear intent and manifest more spirit, vitality, and inspiration. You laugh more, assume less; you are more detached from outcomes and do not take things personally. You take greater responsibility for everything that happens. You pay attention and learn by observing. When you act, you act with lightning speed, without hesitation.

Invisible power is internal; it doesn't manifest in many outward signs, as visible power does, but you can sense it in certain qualities:

Signs of Invisible Power at Work

- A quiet demeanor
- A quiet, assured self-confidence
- Respect toward others
- Without being rude, no strict adherence to protocol
- Good-natured sense of humor
- Unpretentiousness
- Commanding presence
- Natural leadership
- Ability to end conversations or meetings
- Simplicity in dress
- Ease and comfort with physical contact and eye contact
- Comfort in any setting

Signs of Invisible Power in Communication

- Speaks with authority but also compassion
- Is creative and skillful with people and problems
- Smiles with the eyes
- Treats everyone equally without regard for position or status
- Asks questions that lead to discovery (Socratic method)
- Has direct and yet compassionate honesty

- Speaks clearly and simply in words everyone can understand

In terms of physical situation, the holder of invisible power clears away physical obstacles and barriers in order to deal with others directly.

Symbols of Invisible Power at Work

As for displaying symbols of invisible power, the possessor of this power needs no props, uniforms, or impressive surroundings and will adopt them only if protocol or others demand them.

You cannot fake having invisible power; you either have it or you don't. If you don't have it, you can acquire it.

You can, however, fake having visible power, but it will eventually lead to a downfall, so it's never a good idea to even attempt it. People who function on the basis of external power alone are always fearful. People who have acquired some invisible power may be fearful, but it doesn't prevent them from reaching their goals. Once you have acquired enough invisible power, you are no longer fearful: You are free.

SUMMARY

Important Concepts to Remember

- Visible power has signs and symbols that are culturally determined.

- You can appear powerful for a time using only visible forms of power, but the power will be short-lived and easily overturned by one who uses both forms.
- In business, there are obvious signs of visible power.
- Invisible power aligns you with the power inherent in a situation.
- When you are using invisible power, you are using the second attention, functioning in the moment from a strong, clear intent.
- A person using invisible power has many identifiable qualities including warmth, compassion, and humor.

Part 3

THE
PATHWAYS
OF POWER

Chapter 15

THE PATH
WITH HEART

When a person knows his or her life purpose, all other
things become balanced and clear.

— Sarangerel, *Riding Windhorses:*
A Journey into the Heart of Mongolian Shamanism

If you look at the great leaders through history, you see
a consciousness of their own limitations that was essential
to their greatness. From Confucius, Buddha, and Christ, to
Lincoln, Gandhi, and Martin Luther King — all touched
lives because of their presence more than their position. They
became archetypes for the right use of power, and one source
of their power was their humility.

— Peter Block, *Flawless Consulting:*
A Guide to Getting Your Expertise Used

RULE 9

All real power has light as its one true source;
the power path that manifests light
is the path of love, the path with heart.

THE PATH WITH HEART

Shamans distinguish between ordinary life paths and what they call the path with heart. Ordinary life paths derive from the first attention, the world of ordinary reality based on social conditioning and imprinting. In this ordinary world you tend to do what is expected of you socially, to follow the dictates of your social class, to work in professions and jobs that promise the most rapid advancement and perks and that lead to the "good life" as defined by your culture. From the shaman's perspective such ordinary life paths, while possibly producing successful results in terms of wealth and status, are paths with limited power. The reason these paths lack power is that they are infused with only a small amount of inner light — and it is *light,* according to shamans, that is the source of all true power.

Shamans prefer a different path, the path of the second attention, the path with brilliant inner light and infinite power, the path with heart: the power path. True shamans would never call this path of power a "career" because, according to them, a career is a social concept that enslaves whoever has it. A career demands certain predictable moves and practices that ensures its success — and ensure the enslavement of the career holder as well. A shaman eschews routines and habits, especially those that lead to a form of enslavement, no matter how attractively packaged. Thus, although a shaman does a shaman's work, it is never called a career. Shamans call what they do their "work of choice," and perhaps the best description of their methods and lives is simply this: they follow the path with heart.

The Nature of the Path with Heart

The path with heart has no set of predictable moves to ensure success. It is not a set of routines or a prescription of step-by-step actions; it is a philosophy, a way of seeing and being in the world that leads you to your life task, the contribution that spirit asks you to make.

To discover the path with heart, you have to be willing to surrender to spirit, to allow spirit to dictate your moves and decisions spontaneously. This way of being is challenging and difficult for most people of the modern world, because we are trained from birth to value what we call freedom and independence. We are taught not to surrender under any circumstances and to fight for what we believe in. While these concepts sound good and have merit, from a shaman's point of view most people are obviously confused about what they believe in, and even if they are clear about it, their beliefs are often not worth fighting for. For a master shaman what is worth fighting for is the freedom to pursue the real power that resides within — the path with heart.

Shamans know that real power comes with a price and that price includes surrendering to what the Toltec shamans call the Eagle. The Eagle is just another name for spirit, the great power of creation that lies behind everything.

To have true power, a shaman must let go of personal attachments and expectations, ego-oriented desires for comfort and success. The path of heart, while extremely satisfying and fulfilling, is not an easy path to follow because it is demanding, requiring sacrifice — a word that shamans don't use very much but allude to a great deal. Their idea of sacrifice is not the same as that described by some religions that teach that suffering is good and heaven the reward for sacrifice. For a shaman, sacrificing for some future place in heaven makes no sense; rather, they sacrifice to gain freedom and the power to serve now, to make the highest contribution that they can. Sacrifice is the willingness to be uncomfortable to gain something valuable. Shamans are willing to endure unimaginable discomfort on their paths to real power.

The Seven Signs of the Path with Heart

To recognize your path with heart, you must read the signs along the way. Seven signs will help you recognize the path with heart.

1. **Early signs:** Signs early in life point to what you are here to do. They show up as certain daydreams or fantasies or in forms of child's play. For hours at a time, when he was small child, a great comedian used to entertain his audience of stuffed animals, telling them jokes and stories. A financial planner used to play store as a child. He organized all the neighbor children to have stores that bought and sold crafts from one

another. Naturally his was the most successful, and he always ended up with all the play money, so he then had to redistribute it to keep the game going. (There is a great lesson in this for the ultra-successful.) A naturalist spent his childhood collecting frogs and reptiles. A famous fashion designer made unique and colorful clothes for her dolls. An anchorwoman used a pretend microphone as a child to report on the goings-on in her household. A physician cleaned scratches and performed fake surgeries on his childhood friends. These are all examples from the lives of real people who have been our clients over the years.

2. Natural talent: As you grow up you may forget these early childhood dreams and try to conform to other social pressures about what you ought to do with your life. In a shaman's view, however, there is always a talent for that which spirit created you to do.

A drama teacher suspected that a failing, gang-oriented student, involved in car thefts and burglary, had some talent for acting. The teacher talked the boy into taking a lead part in the high school play, the role of a con artist. The boy was brilliant and went on to become a successful actor.

3. Doing what you enjoy: Not only do you have talent for what you have been designed to do but you also clearly enjoy doing it when you have the opportunity. A young man whose parents said he loved to argue as a child went on to become a well-known trial lawyer after failing to make the grade as an opera singer. A woman who as a child loved designing dollhouses went

on to become an award-winning architect, after drop-
ping out of medical school.

4. **Allies:** The path with heart always comes with
allies to assist you in finding it when the terrain is
roughest. These allies come in many forms, sometimes
at the most unexpected times. The ally might be a high
school counselor who steers you in the proper direction
or a coach with some insight into your abilities. The ally
might be a relative who provides an opportunity or a
benefactor who picks you out of a crowd to do something special. The drama coach who helped the juvenile
delinquent is a striking example.

Sometimes allies show up to guide you much later
in life, even after a distinguished career in work that
was adequate but not the true path with heart. After a
highly successful career as an astronaut, Edgar Mitchell
founded the Institute of Noetic Sciences in California,
a center that sponsors international conferences on
topics relating science to spirituality.

5. **Unexpected promptings:** The path with heart
comes with unexpected events and situations that steer
you toward it: failure to pass an exam, an unplanned
interview, a spontaneous meeting, getting lost and
ending up in the perfect place, a missed plane, a fortu-
itous encounter on a bus, the loss of a job just in time
to be available for a better one. According to shamans
these events are not accidents. You should expect them
and allow them to clear the way to your destination, the
path with heart. All too often we are so distracted or
clinging so stubbornly to our agenda that we miss the

importance of an event and fail to see it for what it is, a gift from spirit. All too often we resist the workings of spirit and sometimes even feel victimized by unforeseen changes in plans.

Shamans recommend that we give up the scripts, the careful planning that goes into controlling the future, because otherwise we will not have spirit's help. To a shaman, such a controlled life reeks of self-importance. It is as if to say that we know better than spirit what is right. If we insist on approaching life in this way, then we will be blind to spirit's help and won't receive the assistance we need. The result is a carefully scripted and controlled life with no zip, no zest, and no actual power. Nevertheless, a shaman would say help is always on the way, recognized or not.

6. **Synchronistic events, magical moments:** Synchronistic events, magical moments that have no rational explanation, accompany discovery of the path with heart. From a shaman's point of view, they are among the foremost ways to discern the power path.

In the late seventies a senior manager of a large paper manufacturing firm decided to enroll in an EST (Erhard Seminars Training) program, at the time a popular two-weekend consciousness-raising program. As he was arriving at the airport for his flight to New York for the training, he glanced up and was startled to see a large sign proclaiming "NO EST." When he got closer, he chuckled to see that the sign actually read "NORTHWEST," for Northwest Airlines, but a telephone pole had obscured the middle section.

When he arrived at the training seminar in New York, he was refused entry because he didn't get permission from the psychiatrist who had been treating him for mild depression. Terribly upset, he boarded a plane and returned home, where a message waited that an old friend was in town and wanted to meet with him. The meeting resulted in a complete change of life for him. He resigned from his job, moved to Chicago, and enrolled in a training program for computer software development, a fledgling industry at the time. Eventually he became the CEO of a start-up software-manufacturing firm that he sold three years later for over 300 million dollars. Today he heads a highly effective foundation that assists learning disabled children through the use of computer programs. He found his path with heart through a series of synchronistic events.

Now he likes to say that if he had known then what he knows today, he would never have boarded the plane for the training. Just seeing the sign "NO EST" would have been enough to give him the message.

7. **Signs that confirm you are on the path:** When you have arrived at the path with heart, signs will confirm that you are on the right path. You will discover unexpected success, allies, breakthroughs, and all manner of support for doing what you are designed by spirit to do. Signs will be everywhere you are on the path of power.

During a consultation a highly successful director of sales training in a large commercial real estate firm lamented to us that she did not seem to be doing anything in the world to help anyone. She felt that perhaps she should be working as a physician or fundraiser for charitable organizations. She felt guilty that she worked in a corporate setting that did not seem to be making a real difference in the world.

We asked her if she enjoyed her work as head trainer, and she said yes. We asked her if she was good at teaching, and she said yes. We asked her if she was well liked in the position and if people valued her presence there, and she replied affirmatively. We asked her if she had had opportunities presented to her on a regular basis, and she agreed she had. We asked her what about the position she liked best of all, and she said, "Inspiring people and selling them on themselves." She broke into a grin when she realized what she had just said. "I guess I am making a difference, aren't I! I am helping people in a corporate setting. The truth is, I love the work. I just always thought it was supposed to look different."

From a shaman's point of view, there were many obvious signs that this woman was designed by spirit for the work she does. Her guilt, because of social imprinting, simply prevented her from fully enjoying herself.

SUMMARY
Important Concepts to Remember

- Shamans distinguish between ordinary life paths and what they call the path with heart.
- The path with heart has no set of predictable moves or routines that ensure success.

- In order to discover the path with heart, you
  have to be willing to surrender to spirit.
- To have true power, a shaman must let go of
  personal attachments and expectations, ego-
  oriented desires for comfort and success.
- Seven signs can help you recognize the path
  with heart:

  1. Signs early in life point to what you are here
     to do.
  2. You always have a natural talent for what
     spirit created you to do.
  3. You clearly enjoy doing it when you have the
     opportunity.
  4. The path with heart always comes with allies
     to assist you.
  5. The path with heart comes with unexpected
     events and situations that steer you toward it.
  6. Synchronistic events accompany the discov-
     ery of the path with heart.
  7. When you have arrived at the path with
     heart, signs will confirm that you are now on
     the right path, the path with power.

Chapter 16

STAYING ON THE PATH WITH HEART

Listening to the inner voice — trusting the inner voice —
is one of the most important lessons of leadership.

— Warren Bennis, *On Becoming a Leader*

RULE 9 CONTINUED

All real power has light as its one true source;
the power path that manifests light
is the path of love, the path with heart.

OBSTACLES TO THE PATH WITH HEART

Even the path with heart has obstacles; we have already mentioned some of them. Obviously guilt and social imprinting can get in the way of truly surrendering to the path of power, the path with heart. There are other obstacles as well.

In his book *Synchronicity: The Inner Path of Leadership,* Joseph Jaworski, chairman of the Center for Generative Leadership, outlines with exceptional candor some of the major obstacles and traps he discovered on his path with heart. After experiencing tremendous success in founding the American Leadership Forum, he ran into some difficult times because, as he puts it, traps distracted him. He outlines the three main traps that he fell into:

1. **The trap of responsibility**, a belief that he was indispensable to the whole process and project. This caused him to work himself into a frenzy. As a shaman would describe it, he suffered a loss of power owing to self-importance.

2. **The trap of dependency**, relying on other people and the fixed, scripted plan so much that the spontaneous natural process became blocked. A shaman would describe this as a loss of power and a blockage of spirit due to relying on fixed assumptions.

3. **The trap of overactivity or anxiety**, second-guessing and failing to look inside to find that place of power deep within. A shaman would describe this as

losing oneself in the first attention and forgetting to switch to second attention, where the real power is.

Joe was astute enough to learn from his mistakes and take the proper steps to rectify them. In a business world where even the word *heart* is suspect, he clearly understands the path with heart very well.

In addition to these three traps, other obstacles and distractions occur on the path with heart:

4. The trap of distraction: You can become lazy or distracted by the perks of the first attention, such as valuing profits, status, or influence over what spirit wants of you.

5. The trap of self-deception: You can fail to tell the truth to yourself and others. Fooling yourself will cause you to leave the path with heart because it requires the utmost in personal honesty.

6. The trap of negative thinking: You can fall into the trap of negative thinking and become suspicious, cynical, and disparaging.

7. Loss of the vision: You can lose your perspective and, instead of keeping your eye on the big picture and your focus on your destination, shrink your view and get lost in the details, thus obscuring your understanding of the path with heart.

8. Loss of your detachment: You can insist on taking everything personally, thus becoming defensive, resentful, and embittered instead of maintaining a healthy detachment.

9. "Going on automatic": You can lose your attention

and "go on automatic," thus going to sleep, in a sense, and leaving yourself vulnerable to anyone or anything that might attempt to lead you astray from your vision.

10. **The trap of sloppiness and laziness:** You can become sloppy and cease to do your best, failing to give your all in terms of power and energy. Limping along in a half-hearted way, you lose the path with heart and enter another, less powerful path, the path of least resistance, laziness, rigid expectations, or fixed assumptions.

STAYING ON THE PATH WITH HEART

How do you manage to dodge the traps and obstacles and stay on your path with heart? There are truly thousands of ways, many of them sprinkled throughout this book. Here are a few of them.

When Joseph Jaworski writes about the traps he fell into as he followed his vision, he also gives the antidotes he discovered to become free of the traps. Based on his own experience, he suggests:

1. Keep your perspective.
2. Stay flexible.
3. Go within.

Miguel Ruiz, a shaman and trained physician with family roots in the Toltec shamanic tradition, writes in his book *The Four Agreements* about four primary personal practices or rules that, if followed, will automatically help you stay on the path with heart, the power path. These four agreements appear to be very simple, but they require a tremendous amount of discipline to carry out. These four agreements are in keeping with the philosophy of shamans all over the world:

1. Be impeccable with your word.
2. Don't take anything personally.
3. Don't make assumptions.
4. Always do your best.

Theun Mares, an African shaman originally from Zimbabwe, offers other suggestions for staying on the path with heart in his *Return of the Warriors*. He observes the following:

1. People of knowledge must pay attention to the details of life, for it is the accumulation of all the small things that create our entire worldview.
2. A shaman must intend — must *want* — to be highly aware. This intention causes intensified perception that then generates much greater power.
3. A shaman must change his or her ways of thinking or doing whenever the path of power requires it. At times changes must be

made immediately and radically. Necessary change allows no compromises.

4. A power hunter must be constantly observant and aware of the small, apparently insignificant acts initiated by either the hunter or the prey; these small, minor acts can trigger major changes in perception and awareness.

All these writers from various traditions around the world draw from the same knowledge base — the shamanic tradition — in their observations about staying on the path with heart. They all point to the importance of remaining flexible, telling the truth, avoiding expectations, attending to the little things, harnessing the power of intention, heightening awareness, being impeccable, taking responsibility, contributing your best effort and more.

THE PATH WITH HEART AND BUSINESS LEADERSHIP

With its complex organizations and endless dealing, the world of business is a vast and intensified arena where you can learn shamanic lessons rapidly and accrue power quickly. Like the hunt, it is a high-stakes game where you can easily become distracted and lose the power path without even realizing it. Only when you suffer some grim consequences are you reminded that you have stepped off the path.

In this fascinating playing field many players use only the first attention. Because they see the world from this one frame of reference, they simply do not see anything relating to another frame of reference. They will usually even scoff at any suggestion that there is another way to see, and their hostility can be formidable. They often occupy key positions and can determine the rules of the playing field. They may appear to have power, but in a shamanic context, it is only an illusion. They are actually weaker players, only there to make you stronger — to be your petty tyrant, as Don Juan Matus taught Carlos Castaneda. They are there to challenge your skills and help you to grow, and therefore they represent your opportunity, not your defeat.

Sometimes people who use only the first attention do manage to stumble into their own path with heart, their power path. From a shaman's viewpoint, that is because they are receiving help from spirit, even if they do not recognize or acknowledge it. In this way they may achieve a measure of happiness, satisfaction, and even some real power. Usually, however, the sign a person is using only the first attention is that they are never satisfied, they are unhappy no matter what their lot is, and they do not exhibit the traits of a person on the path with heart.

Fortunately for all of us, many people in the world of business already know how to make use of the second attention, who are discovering or have already found their power path, and who have begun to accrue some real power. A shaman would say these people are identifiable and noticeable to another who "sees" because they literally shine with light and exhibit a powerful inner strength. They often have to battle systems, policies, and management that are oppressive and extremely limited in vision and understanding. All too often they must function in a world where fear-based decision making reigns supreme and people's fear patterns appear to be in control much of the time. These conditions only temporarily deter them because, being on the power path, the path with heart, they have tasted a reality that is incomparable to any other way of being, and once setting foot on this path, there is no turning back.

Each day, as more people discover the power path by one method or another, the ratio between people on the path with heart and those not on the path changes, and the balance of power shifts to those on the power path. This relentless change in balance is already being felt in all aspects of the business and organizational worlds, from frontline workers all the way to the highest echelons of management. Like the gradual change of seasons, this inevitable movement is not noticeable on an hourly or daily basis, but it is clearly apparent from a longer range view. Those caught napping will either be brought along at some point or will find themselves in a world that they increasingly do not understand or find comfortable.

As the balance continues to shift, substantial, powerful changes take place in how business is conducted.

The Future of Organizations and the Path with Heart

Here are some of the future trends that will become more established as the path with heart becomes more widespread. Some are already noticeable in many organizations.

1. While logic and statistics will not be ignored, more attention will be given to intuition in decision making.

2. More attention will be given to placing people in work that they find meaningful and empowering. And yes, there are people who find janitorial work and changing tires truly meaningful and heartfelt. For most kinds of work, there are those for whom it is a power path.

3. More emphasis will be given to contemplation, reverie, meditation, and rest as powerful contributors to effectiveness and productivity.

4. Without lapsing into superstition, more credibility will be given to inner wisdom, synchronistic events, powerful signs, and omens.

5. Allies, powerful locations, wilderness, and elements of nature will all be given greater attention in helping to restore and re-empower a depleted workforce.

6. Natural alliances will be encouraged and abrasive partnerships will be dismantled even faster than they are today based on a deeper shamanic understanding.

7. Skills training for many types of jobs will include heightened awareness exercises, training in "seeing" and the second attention, and shamanic techniques for hunting power and eliminating power-losing practices.

8. More emphasis will be placed on creating power teams that work in balance and are maximally effective.

SUMMARY

Important Concepts to Remember

- Obstacles to the path with heart include:

  1. The trap of responsibility
  2. The trap of dependency
  3. The trap of overactivity or anxiety
  4. Distraction
  5. Self-deception
  6. Negative thinking
  7. Loss of the vision and getting lost in the details
  8. Loss of detachment
  9. "Going on automatic"
  10. Sloppiness and laziness

- Tools for staying on the path with heart
  include:

  1. Keeping your perspective
  2. Staying flexible
  3. Going within
  4. Being impeccable with your word
  5. Not taking anything personally
  6. Not making assumptions
  7. Always doing your best
  8. Paying attention to the details of life
  9. Intending (wanting) to be highly aware
  10. Being willing to change
  11. Being constantly observant and aware of
     small, apparently insignificant acts

- Fortunately for all of us, many people in
  business already know how to make use of
  the second attention, are discovering or have
  already found their power path, and have
  begun to accrue some real power.

Chapter 17

THE FOUR ASPECTS
OF COMMUNICATION

As Serge Kahili King believes, power comes from within, and its source is in fundamental values (*Urban Shaman*, 1990). It's rare that the courage to speak as did a Kennedy or a Gandhi appears in the business world. The danger of appearing foolish or dreamy seems so real and the need to survive so paramount that leaders' deeply held values are often muffled in the face of politics, competition, economics, and desire for dignity in a world where the social reality is that short-term numbers are what really count.

— Charles E. Smith, *The Merlin Factor:*
Keys to the Corporate Kingdom

RULE 8

All power manifests through four aspects:
breath, light, sound, and intent; these aspects form
the basis of communication.

For a shaman, every word spoken is a test of impeccability. A shaman understands how powerful words can be in influencing an outcome and determining awareness. The four aspects of the manifestation of power, breath, light, sound, and intent, form the basis of communication, and how you communicate determines the results you get from the power path.

Let us take a look at how these four aspects work together to create a shaman's most powerful instrument, the power tool of communication.

1. Breath

Breath is the primary vehicle for human sounds and, according to shamanic understanding, is what infuses words with spirit. As you speak, you draw in breath to give power to language, to make words carry to where they will be heard. The breath is the foundation of language and makes communication possible. Written words alone do not have as much power as the spoken word. A poor actor can slaughter the words of Shakespeare and a good one can render them sublime. It is the speaker and not what is spoken that has the greatest power, as anyone who has heard a good public speaker can attest.

What a speaker does with the breath is all important, because breath is not only essential to life, it is also the fuel for the engine of words. Shamans understand breath to be the vehicle that spirit uses to empower life in the human form; breath connects overlapping energy fields, joining them to form body, mind, and spirit. Breath is one of the shaman's principal healing tools; he or she uses it to suck illness out and breathe wellness in. Breath is used to retrieve things that are missing —

including soul retrieval — and to restore harmony and integrity in a patient. Shamans can use breath to move power and energy from one place to another, and they can even infuse power and energy into another person — this is done for healing and sorcery as well. Breath can change a person's perspectives, moods, and conditions.

2. Light

For the shaman, the breath is the carrier of light, the source of all power in the universe. The deeper, purer, and stronger the light carried on the breath, the greater the power of the shaman.

In the shamanic tradition, everything is ultimately light, a deep inner light that master shamans find indistinguishable from love. In the Toltec tradition of shamanic knowledge, spirit is called the eagle and light is the eagle's emanations. The emanations are light waves that spirit uses to create life in every particle of the universe. Every particle then has the power to manifest itself in whatever way it so chooses, and that is why there is such great variety in the universe.

Human beings can become conscious of this power to create from choice, or they can remain largely unconscious of it. Awareness of it is where real power becomes available.

3. Sound

Sound, of course, is an infinite set of frequencies or vibrations that enable the mystery of song and speech to be experienced. Sound conveys both thought and feeling in a great variety of intensities that give rise to endless choices in how you wish to communicate. Sound changes the meaning of words, rendering them serious, lighthearted, humorous, insulting, sarcastic, or filled with praise.

Shamans understand sound as much more than spoken words. Spirit songs for healing and ceremony often have no intelligible words, but shamans have been known to use them to bring rain to a parched land, pull in the herd for a good hunt, or eliminate a virus that has sickened a villager. The strange and beautiful sounds made by shamans create harmonic vibrations within the environment that then enables them to influence it according to their will and intent.

Sound, then, is what transforms the light carried by breath and manifests its power in form. Through the magical act of making sound, shamans say that any person has the power to impact the environment for good or ill.

4. Intent

Intent is the wish or desire that influences the power of the breath to do work and to manifest in a particular way. Without intent, the breath merely keeps the body alive. Intent drives the breath into accomplishment — to communicate, to heal, or to create. Intent drives the light that rides on the breath to go where the shaman wishes it to go. This is what shamans see as the creative process, the actualizing power of the human being made possible by spirit.

THE POWER OF WORDS

Words and language refine the process of manifestation. While words are not required to manifest the power to alter reality, they help a great deal by making our focus and intent more clear. A shaman can heal without words, simply by using breath, sound, and the intention to heal. But words have a power of their own, the power to define, clarify, and focus meaning. Each aspect of power — breath, light, sound, and intent — has some power of its own but when combined, their power becomes enormous. This is the power that shamans believe human beings have available to them day by day, moment by moment, often without even realizing it. When we truly realize the power of our words to create and make things happen, we can never again feel a victim of life or even choose to use words in foolish ways.

How you use words and language indicates your belief system about the world, and your belief system determines whether you are hunter or prey, creator or victim, powerful or weak.

Communication is, then, ultimately intent-driven light using the vehicle of breath and given form through sound. Shamans say that the responsibility of communication is great indeed because through it you have a powerful impact on the world. Through language you determine what your life will be like, whether it is satisfying or painful, fulfilling or disappointing, filled with trust or suspicion, inspired by confidence or driven by fear.

Shamanic Guidelines for Handling Speech

Since speech is so powerful — literally a power tool — shamanic tradition suggests certain guidelines for handling it well:

1. Limit what you say and not engage in talk for talk's sake. Meaningless talk scatters power and renders you weaker. Filling awkward spaces with talk out of nervousness or anxiety leads, in a shamanic sense, to dangerous territory, such as putting others down or gossiping about them. This not only damages them but also creates a reciprocal reaction that will bring the same kind of damage back to you from an unknown source.

2. Say only what you mean. That is, when you speak, be aware of what you say and make sure it is what you believe. Imprecise speech can result in imprecise results. If you say, "The guys in that department are all jerks," is that really what you believe? Will you be forced later to recant and say that you didn't really mean to say that? A good rule is to say something about someone only if you would be willing to say it to that person's face.

If you say to a colleague, "You're looking good for being such an old man," what are you actually saying? Do you mean you're fond of him and are trying to tell him that? Do you dislike him and wish to hide the dislike in a joke? Are you trying to insult him by suggesting he is too old to do his job? What do you actually mean by your words? Say what you mean and your communication will be successful.

Perhaps you are trying to encourage an employee who has been turning in substandard work. You seem to offer approval instead of pointing out what needs revision. When a colleague offers a suggestion for a new approach to handling incoming calls, you secretly disagree but outwardly appear to encourage the idea. You claim to have a project well in hand when you know that it is way behind schedule and you have lost control of it. These are all examples of imprecise communication that can lead to very negative results.

3. Pay attention to what you habitually say and observe if that is what you want to have happen or if you are talking yourself into self-defeat. For example, if you are in the habit of saying, "I can't do it," then soon you won't in fact be able to do it. If you say, "I always fail," then you will always fail. If you say, "I can't seem to ever get a raise," then you won't get a raise. If, on the other hand, you say, "I've had some difficulty, but now I'm ready to succeed," then you will. A good idea is to acknowledge a past condition and then go beyond it, affirming what you want to happen.

4. Pay attention to *how* you speak. Is there a whine in your voice or a complaint? Do you sound bored, exhausted, lethargic? If you feel fatigued or unenthused, be aware that your way of speaking might, despite your wishes or efforts, reveal your condition or

feelings. For a shaman, sound and intent are more important than actual words, and you must realize the power of how you speak; denying anger or uninterest when your way of speaking expresses otherwise will have little effect.

These four simple shamanic guidelines for handling speech can revolutionize business practice all by themselves. Simply attending to speech, reducing the sloppiness around it, and aligning words with intent resolves confusion, enhances clarity and efficiency, and empowers all parties involved in the communication.

Observing your own and others' approaches to communication can reveal many hidden agendas. What you will see is that too often people in business use speech to deliberately obscure, mislead, and distract from the truth. Paying attention to speech and its abuses in a business setting is an exercise worth its weight in gold.

SUMMARY

Important Concepts to Remember

- For a shaman, every word spoken is a test of impeccability.
- All power manifests through four aspects — breath, light, sound, and intent. These form the basis of communication.
- Words and language refine the process of manifestation.

- How you use words and language indicates your belief system about the world, and your belief system determines whether you are hunter or prey, creator or victim, powerful or weak.
- Four shamanic guidelines for handling speech well are:

  1. Limit what you say.
  2. Say only what you mean.
  3. Pay attention to what you habitually say.
  4. Pay attention to how you speak.

Following these guidelines in a business setting can be critical to success.

Chapter 18

THE THREE PRIMARY STYLES OF COMMUNICATION

Alienation is one of the many faces of modernity. The cure is communication and community — a new sense of togetherness. By opening to each other, we diminish the pressure of being alone and exiled.

— Malidoma Patrice Somé, *Of Water and Spirit:*
Ritual Magic in the Life of an African Shaman

RULE 8 CONTINUED

All power manifests through four aspects:
breath, light, sound, and intent;
these aspects form the basis of communication.

Different styles of communication, though only dimly perceived by the average person, nevertheless make a huge difference in determining the clarity and effectiveness of the communication. Shamans the world over recognize that people are not alike in the way they attempt to communicate and in the way they respond to one another. Shamans therefore devise many different strategies for dealing with people of different styles.

The three primary communication styles are often called — simply and clearly — "head," "heart," and "gut," referring to whether an intellectual, emotional, or action orientation marks the style.

Don Juan, shaman-teacher of Carlos Castaneda, recognized that Carlos was primarily a head-oriented person, and so he allowed Carlos to take notes; but at the same time, he would often deliberately frustrate him by forcing him to use other communication styles as a way to teach him balance.

Head People

The head person is intellectually oriented, thinks in words, is concerned with detail, and prefers to use logic and reasoning for problem solving. Head people are slower to process information because they must think things over before coming to a conclusion. They excel at breaking ideas down into their component parts to be sorted, compared, and ordered. They rule the educational system in the United States today, control the media, and generally control how things get done in the business world at this time.

Heart People

The heart person, by contrast, is more aware of the entire field of perception. While the head person is more focused on details and one thing at a time, a heart person grasps many things at once and can sense the gestalt of what is happening. Heart people gather information by how things feel and are good at sensing shapes, forms, textures, colors, sounds, and emotions. Like Einstein, they often grasp the final answer before they understand the logical steps to get to it. They often feel at a disadvantage in North America because their method of communication is not as respected as that of the head type. In other parts of the world, like Brazil, their style is more accepted and influential.

Gut People

The gut person is altogether different, preferring to communicate through actions, by doing things, and by brief signs — the way a basketball player might relay messages about intended actions to fellow team members. A nod of the head, a burst of action, a downward motion of the hand are rapid and sometimes brilliant ways of communicating a great deal of information.

Gut people often eschew words and find emotions to be obstacles to effective action. Another metaphor for this type is the fighter pilot, who, in the heat of battle, does not have time to elaborate a detailed plan of action or consider the aesthetics of a hostile aircraft: the pilot survives by taking instinctive, immediate action.

Communicating between Styles

When head, heart, and gut people meet in the workplace, the potential for miscommunication is enormous. Misunderstanding is not uncommon, and each has a tendency to think their style is the correct one and the others are wrong. The head person has a tendency to think that the heart person is too sentimental and sloppy and that the gut person is inarticulate and dense. The heart person might judge the head person to be cold, aloof, and disengaged and see the gut person as abrupt and disengaged from their feelings as well. Gut people may think of head people as nerds who needlessly complicate things, and they find heart people to be overly emotional and unfathomable. The result is often judgment and bad blood between the styles, which obviously is not good for business. By learning about the different styles and by appreciating the validity and the intricacies of each, communication and cooperation can improve dramatically. This requires some attention and objective study of oneself and others.

Sequence of Styles

Although each person tends to primarily display one of these styles, everyone has all three operating in them all the time; they tend, however, to follow a different order for each person. This means, in effect, there are six different kinds of people trying to communicate with each other in the workplace. Let us look at this a little more closely.

1. Head	2. Heart	3. Gut
1. Head	2. Gut	3. Heart
1. Heart	2. Head	3. Gut
1. Heart	2. Gut	3. Head
1. Gut	2. Head	3. Heart
1. Gut	2. Heart	3. Head

Some head people move to their heart second and their gut last, while other head people move to their gut second and their heart last. These two styles are quite different from one another, as are the other combinations of the styles. To explain the differences, we've found two laws that determine whether or not a particular style is effective.

Law 1: The Second Style Is a Trap

Whichever style a person operates from second will prove unsuccessful in meeting a challenge or solving a problem, and the person will become trapped in the secondary style without making progress.

Because of culture, childhood imprinting, and natural proclivities, people tend to be strongest in one style and habitually lead from it. The next strongest style comes secondarily, and their weakest style comes last. People tend to use their strongest style well for obvious reasons. However, their second style is weaker so they do not use it as well. In fact, this second style often surfaces when they are under stress. A normally head-oriented person may slide into movement (gut) under pressure. Because it is a secondary style they make mistakes with it. The most obvious mistake is to use the second style in service to the first style. For example: Let us say that a head person slides into action under stress. Instead of productive action, they are likely to apply their action to their thoughts and go around and around in their heads, obsessively trapped like a hamster on a wheel. This is often referred to as "analysis paralysis" in the business world. What seems like action is not really action. They are not thinking well any longer nor are they acting productively.

Let us take a second example. A normally heart-oriented person slides to their head under pressure. They try to use their thinking to second-guess their feelings and get trapped there. This usually ends up disastrously because now they are neither having clear feelings nor thinking well. Thus when a person slides ineffectively to their secondary style, they lose the ability to use both their primary style and their secondary style well.

Bear in mind that under ordinary circumstances a person can use all three styles productively and effectively, especially if they are not too imbalanced in the use of one or another style. In the best of worlds, a healthy person thinks when thinking is needed, feels when feeling is most appropriate, and can take effective action when that is called for. The trap occurs when they are considerably less comfortable with the secondary style and when they are under stress.

Law 2: The Third Style Is the Balancer

The third style is the one that can restore balance in a situation and can provide freedom from the trap of the second style. If a head type operates secondarily from the heart, he or she will finally resort to gut and take an action that will provide balance and a solution to the problem or challenge. Interestingly, the third style, the one a person resorts to last, they usually handle well when it finally surfaces. That is why it functions as the balancer, the style that sets things right again. Two real-life examples follow.

Cathy is the CFO of a national trucking company. She excells at her job and manages finances so well that the company has shown profit eight years in a row. She is intellectually centered, can become trapped in her emotions, and is balanced by taking action. Recently she got into a quarrel with the head of acquisitions over whether to retire part of the fleet and update it with the purchase of twelve new trucks. She felt the current fleet had two more years before requiring replacement. Secretly she felt the acquisitions manager was making a power play to raise his stature in the company but risking the well-being and security of the company in the process. She could not figure out a simple solution to the power struggle, and so she went home night after night trapped with worry and anxiety.

After a week of losing sleep, she realized that she was stuck and getting nowhere fast. She decided to take action and prepare a detailed report, call a meeting with the senior management, and outline the financial consequences of three options: (1) buying twelve trucks now, (2) buying three trucks now and the rest in a year, or (3) waiting and buying all the trucks after two years. At the meeting it was decided to go with a combination of options two and three, purchasing three trucks now and the rest in two years. This met with her approval and gave the acquisitions manager something to feel good about as well. The meeting was a success because it was informative, objective, and did not point any fingers at anyone.

Cathy used her action — her gut — to free her from the trap of her emotions, and this returned her to what she does best, think. Her story shows how a head person can become trapped in feeling and get nothing done, whereas decisive action will bring release from the trap and the solution to the problem.

Don is the head of creative design at a large apparel manufacturing firm. He has excellent rapport with people in all departments and a great feel for fashion, design, and current trends. Don is emotionally or heart centered, acts secondarily, and goes to his intellect last. Although he is excellent at what he does, operating secondarily from the gut sometimes creates difficulties.

On one occasion he helped design an exquisite line

of clothing and, without realizing it, selected material that was beautiful but that stained easily and was difficult to clean. He went ahead and ordered great supplies of the material without thinking it through, and although his feel for the design was right on target, he did not consider all the ramifications of his selection of material. When this was pointed out to him, he understood his mistake, canceled the order, and immediately researched materials that were both aesthetic and easy to clean.

Resorting finally to more detailed thinking — to a head style — relieved Don of the gut trap and solved the immediate problem, which in turn restored Don to a favored position in the company and allowed him to carry on successfully with his design work.

SUMMARY

Important Concepts to Remember

- Three primary communication styles are head, heart, and gut.
- Each person possesses all three styles and operates from them in a particular order.
- The rules of sequences are that (1) whichever style a person chooses second will prove unsuccessful in meeting a challenge or solving a problem and (2) the style that is resorted to third will restore balance and provide freedom from the trap of the second style.

Chapter 19

THE POWER OF TEAMS

Transformation is the process of experientially invalidating and letting go of beliefs that no longer serve a constructive purpose....[T]he realization that a team's success is more important than an individual's personal success is a radical shift for someone who has valued, practiced, and been rewarded for rugged individualism most of his or her life.

— William A. Guillory,
The Living Organization — Spirituality in the Workplace

RULE 2 CONTINUED

Power stems from four primary sources:
(1) inspiration; (2) simplicity; (3) exchange;
and (4) conception.

In the twenty-first century the business world is the arena where most people choose to play the game of accumulating power. If, when striving to gain or hold onto power, individuals perceive a setting as hostile, they will act independently and perhaps work against others. They will often compete for the available power like ten-year-olds grabbing for the last few slices of pizza on the table. If, on the other hand, they sense a setting is congenial, they will join together and cooperate to form power teams, knowing they can gain more power by functioning as a group than by struggling independently. Shamans understand that groups of people working together naturally draw power to themselves. Working in teams is more inspiring than working alone, can simplify the workload, provides an avenue of exchange, and therefore supports conception of new ideas and methods.

From a shaman's point of view, a successful enterprise will set up an environment to draw its members into power teams, and certain natural configurations attract more power than others.

The Power of Numbers

In a shamanic way of seeing the world, the number of a group's members multiplied by itself determines its power. Thus one person working alone has the power of one; a group of two has a power of four — quadruple the energy, strength, inspiration, influence, and ability of one. A group of three has the power of nine, and so on — with each added person the strength goes up by a quantum leap.

Indigenous peoples are group oriented because they have learned the strength that comes with numbers.

Medicine people typically invite the entire family, clan, or tribe to participate in a healing ceremony because they know how much stronger the effects will be with the added participants.

Considering the shamanic formula of power as the square of the number of group members, obviously a large corporation with thousands of employees has the potential for vast power. Potential power, however, is typically not realized or is squandered because of divided loyalties, divisive policies, lack of coordination, poor communication, lack of vision and shared philosophy, and many other power-eroding factors. Although not free of power-eroding practices, the Japanese have succeeded at uniting large groups of people under a single philosophy, and this has proven advantageous to business.

Despite the great potential power of large groups, however, smaller groups are generally more successful at establishing cohesiveness and therefore more effective than larger groups. Smaller groups tend to move more quickly and agilely than large ones. What truly strengthens and empowers smaller teams, however, are the seven elements listed below. As you review them, you can see why it is far more challenging to get a large group of people to manifest all these qualities than to get a small group working together.

Shamanic Elements of Cohesion

These seven elements are crucial in building a team and making it a highly effective power group:

1. To be powerful, a group must share a common philosophy or set of values.

Something must connect people to their teammates. People who agree on what is important feel connected.

Key words: agreement, connection

2. They must perceive the group intent as worthwhile enough to get their interest for a considerable time investment.

The goal must be compelling enough to motivate people to commit to go the distance with the team.

Key words: intent, commitment

3. The group must commonly perceive that working together brings more empowerment than working independently.

Each team member must see enough of the big picture to understand the value of the endeavor and what it means for them personally.

Key words: viewing the big picture

4. They each must perceive their teammates as friendly or supportive to their own personal power, not hostile or competitive.

Members of a team must trust their teammates and feel supportive of each member's success. Feeling trust and support of course does not mean teammates will not disagree vociferously about certain points. Friendly conflict can be very useful in pushing the group to the edge of chaos in their thinking process. Self-organizing systems arise in such contexts.

Key words: trust, support

5. They must be willing to selflessly give up some of their own gratification and personal power building for the sake of contributing to a greater power that they will then all benefit from.

Team participants must be willing to serve a higher cause, to give of themselves, to create something more powerful than they could manage alone.

Key words: selflessness, contribution

6. They must come to the team with a level of personal power that matches their team members' power.

Teams are successful when they are composed of equals — not necessarily in skills or ideas but in the capacity for holding, handling, and generating power. Working together as equals creates genuine trust and respect for one another. Remember that the shaman's definition of power is *to be able, to have potential, and to have the vigor or energy to do.*

Key words: equality, respect

7. They must be able to communicate with one another effectively.

Even if all the other elements are present, if team members cannot communicate with one another, they will be ineffective. Communication depends on a willingness and commitment to fundamentally understand one another. Successful, powerful communication depends on the presence of the six other elements.

Key words: communication, understanding

SUMMARY

Important Concepts to Remember

- Certain natural team configurations attract power.
- In a shamanic way of seeing the world, the number of a group's members multiplied by itself determines its power.
- Smaller groups tend to be more cohesive and more agile.
- Seven elements crucial in building a team and making it a highly effective power group are:

  1. A common philosophy or set of values.
  2. A compelling goal.
  3. A common perception that working together brings more empowerment than working independently.
  4. A supportive setting.
  5. Willingness to sacrifice personal power building and gratification for the sake of a greater benefit to the whole group.
  6. They must come to the team with a level of personal power that matches their team members' power.
  7. They must communicate with one another effectively.

Chapter 20

TEAM CONFIGURATIONS

Since all creation is a whole, separateness is an illusion. Like it or not, we are all team players.

— John Heider, *The Tao of Leadership*

RULE 2 CONTINUED

Power stems from four primary sources:
(1) inspiration; (2) simplicity; (3) exchange;
and (4) conception.

In this chapter, we focus on the third and fourth primary sources of power: exchange and conception. In any organization, effective exchange and conception of new ideas involve building a team.

The number of individuals composing a team makes a huge difference in how that team will operate. Indigenous leaders know a great deal about the inherent power in specific numbers, and they often use configurations deliberately in forming groups of apprentices, for example. Here we will discuss the properties of different sizes of small teams and the different attributes of each. We need to focus only on teams of twelve or less, because every effective large group is composed of small teams.

General Principles

- Even-numbered teams are more stable than odd-numbered teams and are therefore good for long-term projects and ongoing situations.
- Teams of an odd number tend to be unstable and are therefore usually undesirable for long-term purposes. However, an odd-numbered team is often very effective when the objective is, for example, to break new ground. Although odd numbers create stress, that stress is sometimes useful and necessary for growth.
- Even if individual team members come and go, maintaining a stable number of players is important; to ensure success, keep the size of a team the same over time.

- A team may be composed of people of widely different educational and skill levels or training: the errand runner or gofer is just as important as the manager or lead lawyer.
- Large teams, such as whole departments, tend naturally to break down into smaller groups.

Team of One

One is not a team, unless there are invisible members. Lone shamans often function as a team when they include various allies and helping spirits in their work. For our discussion here, however, we will assume one is usually not a team.

Team of Two

A team of two is a partnership. Although the smallest possible team configuration, partners are powerfully effective when the seven elements of cohesion (discussed above) are present. Two working together have the power of four, and four is a stable number.

Team of Three

Teams of three are usually not effective because they are naturally unbalanced, like three-legged stools. Two form a natural partnership and a third addition to the partnership of two can find it difficult to be included or can even be divisive in an effort to form their own partnership with one of the team members. Power tends to be lost in these dynamics.

Although rare, a set of three can work successfully together if their intent is strong and the members have enough maturity, commitment, and awareness. Sometimes a team of three can be balanced by a fourth who plays a minor part, such as a distant researcher, supplier, or customer.

On a comical note, the Three Stooges appealed to so many people for a reason: the natural imbalance of their team of three helped to create their typically ludicrous and ineffective dynamics.

Team of Four

Teams of four are naturally the most stable, effective, and powerful for most projects and endeavors. The problems and instability of three are easily remedied by adding a fourth member. The advantages of four are apparent in a great many other arenas as well. When Honda Corporation came out with their three-wheeled all-terrain vehicles, they were immensely popular, but there were so many rollovers that involved critical injuries and deaths that lawsuits proliferated. Eventually Honda took them off the market and replaced them with four-wheeled ATVs, and the accident rate plummeted.

Teams of four naturally break into four fields or positions. Each position contributes a unique power to the whole. The four positions are characterized by these qualities:

1. Initiative
2. Knowledge

3. Power

4. Support

No matter who comprises the group of four, each member of the team will always gravitate toward one of these four positions. Naturally, by selecting talented individuals for each spot, you can greatly accelerate the effectiveness of the team — and if you place four of the same or similar types on a team, they will have more difficulty than a team composed of different personality types.

It sometimes happens that members rotate between positions, filling the initiative position one day and the knowledge spot another, for example. Teams of four can be flexible in this manner, but usually they fall into a typical pattern. Let's examine the four positions in detail.

1. Initiative: This spot is held by the initiator, the team member who comes up with the original ideas, the one to first propose something, to make initial suggestions. The initiator may not necessarily know how to implement the task, but they are first to propose it. The initiator tends to be creative, confident, and flexible in style, often bringing up more ideas than the group can possibly implement.

2. Knowledge: The person in the knowledge position is the one who researches the merit or potential of a proposal and discovers what is required to achieve it. They supply valuable information to either validate or contradict the proposal. People in this spot tend to be curious, information and detail oriented, and in need of ideas that get them into action.

3. **Power:** The power position is a natural for someone who is results oriented. The person who fills this spot is eager to move into the action phase and tends to propose the steps toward action, create the timetable, and motivate the team to take the first necessary steps. The person in the power position is usually a confident, can-do type. This type is also good at knowing which other players need to get involved to make an idea happen more quickly.

4. **Support:** Finally, there will always be that member of the team who naturally fills the support position best, helping the team remain cohesive and providing inspiration to the rest of the group. The person in this position often does the bulk of the grunt work because they are willing to do whatever is necessary to ensure a project's success. The support person finds the meeting place, provides the materials, notifies everyone of the time and place, and even feeds the crew, if necessary. Although often less esteemed and rewarded, this position is vital to the group's effectiveness; in fact, the group cannot function without this person's contribution.

A power team is usually made up of a group of four individuals, but often when the team is central to a business, groups grow up around each individual and the positions in turn become departments. Team members may themselves become part of a new team of four. The knowledge person may head up the research department or perhaps the legal department and consequently occupies a position on that new team. The knowledge person on team one might also occupy the power position on team two. The team positions and departments that tend to grow up around them are

1. Initiative: development; marketing.
2. Knowledge: research; legal; training; ethics.
3. Power: production; manufacturing; accounting; financing.
4. Support: sales; human resources; general organizational effectiveness; secretarial; janitorial; supplies.

Team of Five

A group of five is unbalanced and less stable than a group of four. Nevertheless, a team composed of five individuals can be quite powerful if it has a special, time-limited mission. While five is not a team number designed for longevity, in the short run it can accomplish a great deal.

A team of five has the four positions described above plus one more, the powerful "eccentric." The eccentric is an original voice, a variant, one who contributes something unique to the stable functioning of the basic four. The "fifth wheel" is often an unusual character who introduces and motivates the team with unconventional ideas, unusual approaches, and uncommon enthusiasm. Sometimes a team of four will resist their inclusion, seeing the eccentric as intrusive or strange. Other times, however, this position is welcomed as the necessary element for blazing a new trail or firing up productivity. When the intent of the group is strong and the purpose very clear, the fifth member can add a big power boost to create an out-of-the-box effect and make a quantum leap in a new direction. The bigger the project, the more useful the eccentric.

Most eccentrics are highly creative and flexible individuals who take a nonlinear approach to problem solving. They can be difficult to understand at first, but their ideas are often signs of pure genius.

Team of Six

A team of six is, like its four-member counterpart, stable and productive. Although not as efficient and fast as a team of four, what it lacks in mobility it gains in expertise. In addition to the five positions outlined above, there is a sixth position, the integrator. The integrator is a highly confident individual who knows how to interface with the world at large. This person knows how to take the ideas created by a team of five and make them acceptable to the whole company, the media, and the public by putting a legitimate, authoritative spin to them. They are often power brokers and entrepreneurial types who move from situation to situation, making deals, creating results, and then moving on to the next exciting challenge. Sometimes they are brought aboard as the CEO or a similar position on the upper management team. Teams of six are common and exceptionally effective at producing results.

Team of Seven

Teams of seven are rare and belong in the category of the unstable groups of three and five. A team of seven is designed less for taking on everyday projects and much more for handling large undertakings that may involve the general public or that will affect an entire business field. As with the other odd-numbered teams, a very strong intent and clear vision are necessary to hold a team of seven together and produce effective results.

The seventh position on this team is the observer, a member who acts as a record keeper to the activities of the group and offers wise counsel based on close observation. This member is often a consultant or outside adviser.

Team of Eight

A group of eight people actually comprises two quadrants working together. It has stability and power and is an effective, strong team for getting a job done.

Team of Nine

A group of nine, although made up of an odd number of members, differs from other teams and is an excellent number for a business endeavor such as the creation of a board of directors, an investment group, or a top-level management team. Teams of nine tend to be egalitarian, with leadership and responsibility shared among the team members.

As with the other odd-numbered teams, this group is most viable and strikingly powerful when there is a clear goal, strong intention, and high level of interest. If the interest level falls off or if some of its members get distracted, the team will rather quickly lose its effectiveness and fall apart. The team of nine has the added advantage of having a natural tiebreaker in the event of a vote.

Team of Ten

A team of ten is usually a combination of a team of four and a team of six. Both are stable, and if they work together with common values and goals, the team of ten is generally stable and productive.

Team of Eleven

As an unbalanced team, a group of eleven will usually prove to be clumsy and ineffective in the long run. A team this size is best suited to a short-term objective and can be highly effective in promoting growth and implementing a project that requires pushing the envelope. Members of this relatively large team need discipline and maturity to achieve their objectives.

Team of Twelve

Though large, a team of twelve has distinct strengths. Twelve is the number ideally suited to providing solid support, and this is the team's greatest asset. To name just a few examples of twelve as a support number: Jesus chose twelve apostles to surround himself with; there are twelve signs to the zodiac and twelve months in our calendar year; an octave in modern music has twelve tones; all nation's coastlines have twelve mile fishing limits around them. Teams of twelve are stable and all-inclusive; they have everything they need to be successful and highly cohesive.

A team of twelve can include two teams of six, three teams of four, or one team of six and two teams of three — all highly stable configurations. A group of twelve makes an excellent support system to back up the work of its subteams. In fact, having all the smaller stable teams form part of a larger team of twelve is ideal.

Twelve is an excellent number for creating a board of directors to support a charitable organization or an artistic endeavor like an opera.

SUMMARY

Important Concepts to Remember

- The number of individuals composing a team makes a big difference in how that team will operate.
- Even-numbered teams are more stable than odd-numbered teams and are therefore good for long-term projects and ongoing situations.
- Teams of an odd number tend to be unstable

and are therefore undesirable for long-term
purposes, but are often very effective for
short-term and special objectives. Although
odd numbers create stress, stress is sometimes useful and necessary for growth.

- To ensure success, keep the size of a team the
  same over time.
- A team may be composed of people of
  widely different educational and skill levels
  or training.
- Teams of four naturally break into four fields
  or positions. Each contributes a unique power
  to the whole:

  1. Initiative
  2. Knowledge
  3. Power
  4. Support

- A team of six members is as stable and pro-
  ductive as a team of four.
- Teams of nine are egalitarian and productive.
- Teams of twelve are stable and all inclusive.

Part 4

MANAGING POWER

Chapter 21

CONNECTING FOR POWER

A human being is part of the whole, called by us the "Universe," a part limited in time and space. He experiences himself, his thoughts, and feelings as something separated from the rest — a kind of optical delusion of his consciousness.

— Albert Einstein

RULE 10

The smaller the degree of separation, the greater the power available.

Disconnection and Powerlessness

From a shamanic perspective, the more disconnected and separate you are from the object of your attention, the less power you can obtain from it. Here's a simple example: When you see a group of people as the enemy and regard them with suspicion, they are unlikely to function as allies and help you out in a time of need. You are choosing a course where you will not become more powerful by joining ranks with them; you also must expend power by defending against them and keeping them at bay. When nations fight they lose all possible commerce between them and become involved in mutual destruction. In the end both nations lose real power through the loss of lives, resources, good will, and the potential trade that could have benefited both.

Connecting and Becoming Powerful

To the degree you feel separate from objects around you, you cannot derive power or benefit from them; on the other hand, the more connection you feel with the objects around you, the more power or benefit you can derive from them.

To someone looking at their environment solely through the first attention, a robin showing up on a branch outside a window during a business meeting seems objectively to represent nothing more than a bird on a branch outside the window. It is incidental, outside, and irrelevant to the meeting going on inside. The

two events are held to be entirely separate and therefore
no power is available in their juxtaposition. To someone
viewing the world through the second attention, however, the bird's appearance just at that moment during
the meeting could be highly meaningful. It may be an
ally with a message about what is occurring or being
transacted at that moment in the meeting. By listening
to any messages the bird might have to say at that
moment, power can be accessed and the outcome of the
meeting can shift dramatically.

In most people's view, suggesting a robin's appearance might hold meaning sounds like a child's way of
thinking, the stuff of fairy tales and magic; the concept
seems ludicrous. Most people would dismiss the possibility out of hand. A shaman, however, would see the
choice to dismiss the event as a most unfortunate denial
of an opportunity for help from spirit and a lost opportunity for power building. In the shaman's worldview, the
prey would be lost in the hunt; the meeting would very
likely bumble along to an unsatisfying conclusion, and
no one would benefit from the outcome.

Let's say that someone is proposing, as a cost-
cutting measure, replacement of the current mail-
service provider with a different one. At that very
moment a robin shows up on the branch outside and
looks directly at you. You tune into the second attention
and immediately hear in your mind, "Don't do it." The
message comes simply, bluntly, without explanation.
But let's say you choose to ignore the message. Later,
the new service turns out to be problematic and the

company loses customers over slow delivery, thus resulting in a drop in sales and increased costs.

Imagine, on the other hand, you choose to listen to the bird and now have an opinion of what to do, but with no good explanation for it. You are in a position where you might look like a fool because you can't give good reasons why the plan shouldn't be supported. So you go back into second attention, a process that breaks down barriers, and you mentally ask the bird, "Why not?" and the bird responds with, "Because it's too slow and you'll lose customers. Check their record." Now you have a compelling reason that supports your opinion. You have accessed power by breaking down the degrees of separation.

The rational mind wants to say, "But this is just projection. You're projecting your own opinion onto the bird and making it seem like the bird answered. It's all going on in your head." And to that, the shaman chuckles and replies, "So what?" The rule still applies: The smaller the degree of separation, the greater the available power. You can theorize whatever you want, but the question really is: "Do you want results or not?" If you do, then you might consider at least experimenting with the shamanic approach — and see what happens as a result.

Connecting versus Identifying

We must clarify one point on this subject: To eliminate the separateness between yourself and the environment or an object in it is not the same as identifying with everything in the environment. This type of identification causes the loss of power and is never recommended by shamans. *Connecting,* by contrast, is a way of gaining power and is always a good idea. Here's a simple example to illustrate the difference. If you identify with someone else's problems, say their loss of a contract, then you will suffer along with them as if the loss had been your own. But connecting with the person having the problem — acknowledging them, listening to them, and offering your presence — empowers both the person and yourself at the same time. A person who is acknowledged in this way does not stay in a troubled place very long, and the result will be that your connection with the person will reward you with greater power. To fully understand this, you have to experience it directly.

Connecting means paying attention to what is going on around you and not screening everything out to such a degree that you miss the magic. When we send people on solos in the wilderness, we suggest that, for the twenty-four hours they will be on their own, they pay attention to everything that happens around them, whether it's the presence of a dragonfly, a lizard, a deer, a breeze, or a cloud. We're always amazed at the depth of wisdom our clients access by connecting to their environments for even a brief period of time. They're almost always amazed as well.

Inner Connection

We have so far looked at connecting with external things in our environment. There is another type of connecting that is a great key to power as well: our inner connection.

The Navajos, the largest shamanically based indigenous tribe in the United States have a lot of insight into our inner connection and its effects on our health: They say that good health is a direct result of inner connection and that disconnection is the source of disease, a major loss of power. They say that the human body is like a country where the organs are cities with highways connecting them to each other so that they work smoothly together, in constant communication. When the paths of communication become blocked or obstructed — for any of a great number of reasons — communication with an organ is cut off similar to the way that a quarantine or siege isolates a village from the others. The organ begins to fail and, in turn, all other parts suffer as well. Even if the afflicted part recovers, it can remain out of communication with the rest of the body until it is reconnected deliberately through a ceremony or healing. The road to health and a return to power involve reconnecting the affected part with the others so that separation is eliminated.

The Navajos tell us that trouble brews when you fail to maintain an inner connection and when you become disconnected inside yourself. When your intellect does not connect with your emotions or your emotions with your actions, you become prone to mistakes in judgment and can suffer mental and emotional problems as a result. Inner disconnection is a major power loss, and the greater the degree of separation, the greater the power loss.

The same principle applies equally to any organization. When a department becomes disconnected from the main body of the organization, the result is an overall power loss. Only reestablishing the lines of communication and reconnecting the department to the organization can restore power. This same principle applies to any area where separation exists, whether it be disconnection with a customer, supplier, funding source, or even what might be perceived as a competitor: The greater the degree of separation, the greater the power loss.

Restoring Connection in the Village

The Huichol Indians of Mexico are the only tribe on the continent that we are aware of that fully retained their shamanic culture after the Spanish invaded and conquered the peoples of that land. They accomplished this by hiding in the rugged Sierras, a terrain so difficult, isolated, and hazardous that the Spaniards gave up trying to capture them. To this day their lives are based on the indigenous wisdom they have accumulated for thousands of years.

One of the finest uses of their wisdom is certainly found in the traditions they have developed that bring harmony to the village. One important tradition keeps the people in the village connected by periodically giving attention to anything that has come between them. At specified times they hold all-night ceremonies for the entire village in which, around the fire, each person can confess to Tatawari, the spirit of the fire, all their transgressions toward anyone else. This is done out loud for everyone to hear.

The result is high drama as everyone finds out who stole Juan's goat, who slept with Anita's husband, or who might have wished ill on another. There is much wailing and upset, but by dawn all is forgiven and there are hugs all around and singing, and everyone embraces the new day with great vitality. Balance and connection have been restored in this highly uncomfortable process of truth telling and purging. The people are no longer separate and the village is once again whole.

SUMMARY

Important Concepts to Remember

- The smaller the degree of separation, the greater the power available.
- The greater the separation, the less power is available.
- Anything in the environment can become an ally and support you on your path. For this to happen, you must connect with it.
- Connecting means paying attention to what is going on around you and not screening everything out to the degree that you miss the magic.
- Connecting is a direct way to power.

- The more connection you feel with objects around you, the more power or benefit you can derive from them.
- Being alert is vital to connecting. A robin may have a message for you.
- Inner connecting is as important as outer connecting. Both are sources of power.
- Connecting is healing. Disconnection leads to disharmony.

Chapter 22

ATTENTION, INTENTION, AND RE-INTENDING

Intent is a force that exists in the universe. When sorcerers beckon intent, it comes to them and sets up the path for attainment, which means that sorcerers always accomplish what they set out to do.

— Carlos Castaneda, *The Active Side of Infinity*

RULE 5 CONTINUED

Power can be manifested only when you focus your attention and intention in the present.

The Power of the Now Point

All the indigenous leaders we have met the world over teach that the point of greatest power exists only in the present moment. From this moment of now, you can influence future events by making powerful choices and from this now point you can even influence past events by perceiving them differently.

For shamans, thinking that you are powerful because you once had power in the past or because of all your grand plans for the future is utterly ineffective. Power is only now; it is based on what you are perceiving now, feeling now, thinking now, choosing now, and acting on now. It is now when all ideas generate, all plans hatch, all actions begin. As the ancient Chinese adage states, the journey of a thousand miles begins with a single step. Thinking endlessly about that step is not an act of power. Conceiving of the step is powerful because it is generative in that moment of creation. Taking the step is powerful. The conception and single step can be taken only in moments of now. The now point therefore requires absolute attention.

ATTENTION

Attention is a product of human awareness, the capacity to attend to what is going on internally and externally at all times. While most of us take the matter of attending for granted, for shamans it is the subject of the greatest interest and study. Shamans place a major emphasis on developing the highest qualities of attention — the special ability to focus and concentrate, a skill they cultivate over many years with daily practice and care.

Most of us, on the other hand, pay dearly for our lack of attention, a failure that is not only personally damaging but also costs industry a vast fortune every year through accidents and expensive mistakes. Inattention and distraction take a massive toll on business projects, on human life on the highways, on the quality of our relationships, and on our personal health.

Shamans understand attention has to do not only with focusing but also with where you put your attention, because, as they believe, a significant part of you goes where your attention goes. If you are operating power equipment and your mind is not on your work but on the fishing trip last weekend with your friends, then you are mostly fishing and little of you is at work. These dangerous conditions make performing consistently and well extremely difficult. So, attending to what you are doing, truly being where you are, and focusing in a laserlike way are fundamental rules of shamanic leaders.

Attention of course can be directed inwardly and outwardly, depending on what is required in the moment. A good shaman directs attention both inwardly and outwardly at the same time. This is called having a foot in both worlds. Navigating the outer ordinary world and the inner spirit world or world of imagination — this is the business of the shaman.

INTENT

According to indigenous peoples, understanding the importance of attention cannot be separated from understanding intent, because the two are inextricably entwined. Your attention is where you choose to focus; your intent directs that focus and guides your attention.

Indigenous peoples see intent as the core of reality, the essence of spirit, the foundation of all perception. Shamans say that there is nothing but intent in the universe — the intent to create, to be, to do, and to have. Without intent, there would be no world, no sun and moon, no solar system, no stars and galaxies, no thoughts, no dreams, no creations, no imagination; intent is the basis of anything and everything. To a shaman, the idea that the universe is a random accident without meaning is indescribably absurd — uproariously funny or pitiful in its ignorance.

Shamans think of intent as being like a vast ocean in which everything is floating. Each object in the universe has its own intent to be what it is. An apple has the intent to be an apple, a crow to be a crow, a mountain to be a mountain. Intent means that each thing is being what it was created to be, actively not passively. Each intends to be itself, desiring at some level to be what it is. Each thing is in perfect agreement with the spirit of creation that produced it in the first place and thus participates in its own creation. For shamans then, each thing in the universe is a cocreator with the forces of creation.

Human beings, too, of course are here on earth doing what they are doing because they intend to be — not at the conscious, rational level, but at a much deeper level of awareness. When we are unaware of this deep intent that, in fact, keeps us alive we are diminished in our power to make a difference in the world with our presence. We can learn, however, to focus on our intent to be alive, rationally, consciously, and with full awareness, and this unleashes great power because we align with the creative power of the universe. When we understand this, where we put our attention becomes a matter of great importance.

Working with Intention

If, as shamans say, we humans are cocreators, through the power of our intent, with the creative spirit of the universe, then naturally we as humans must work with intention. Intention is what makes things happen; intention creates substance from the infinite supplies of resources available in the many levels of reality. From these resources, we create experiences, thoughts, visions, feelings, choices, projects, and so on.

For a shaman, no matter what the nature of the experience — good, bad, painful, or pleasurable — humans have a hand in cocreating it with their intention. This is certainly true in the business world as well: Whether our experience is good or bad, we have had a hand in creating that experience through our intention.

If a product line fails, a designer might say, "I never intended this." But if they could see that, by the failure of the product line, they discovered an improvement that would lead to a major success further down the line, they would more readily embrace the failure. At a deeper level the designer intended the outcome to happen exactly the way it happened because, as a shaman knows, there are no accidents, no victims, no randomness in the universe. With this knowledge, by always paying attention to what happens, and keeping intention fully active, a shaman becomes powerful.

If a shaman doesn't like what he or she sees or experiences, they shift their intention to something more fulfilling. From a shaman's point of view, a person who does not hold this perspective can only feel like a victim of circumstances or be dependent on the whim of fickle gods or fate or chance for favors.

A shaman-like manager or business leader, therefore, will always take full responsibility for whatever happens. There is no self-blaming if the results haven't been good, just the knowledge that a stronger, more focused intent is necessary to achieve different results next time.

RE-INTENDING

How do you shift your intention to bring about more fulfilling results? The first step may seem paradoxical: The first step is to accept conditions the way they are now. By accepting what is, you find neutrality, a place of

nonresistance that is essential to cultivate. You eliminate blame, victimization, obsession, fear of the future,
and all the energy leaks that kill off power building.

To find this state of neutrality and to keep coming
back to this state so that it becomes habitual rather than
simply a momentary experience is a great challenge,
for it involves nothing less than erasing — *dumping* —
years of accumulated habit patterns; you have to empty
out what is in your subconscious. There are many
shamanic methods to do this. A simple one is to write
down all your concerns, fears, and negative beliefs that
make you feel you can't change a situation. Keep writing until you have exhausted the subject and have
nothing else to write down.

Once you are emptied of what disempowers you,
you need to build power to intend something new.
Throughout this book are exercises and practices to
build power — you can seek the outdoors, go to a
powerful place or person, think powerful thoughts, or
engage in meditation, concentration, and martial arts.
All these things lead to an awareness of the second
attention, the source of all power. Once you learn to
access this different state of mind, you look at how you
would rather have the situation be. You see it that way,
feel it that way, and finally come to *believe* it can be
the way you envision. You act as if it were that way.
All the while you must continue to accumulate and
store power by doing some of the practices above.
Merely practicing positive thinking will not accomplish the task. A car does not run without fuel, nor do

you. These exercises provide the fuel for your growing power.

One exercise of Salish shamans of the Pacific Northwest is to build a small-scale model of how you want your situation to be, similar to the way an architect builds a model of a planned building or project. They use pinecones, bark, pebbles, grasses, and anything they can find locally to construct their model. You can use magazine pictures, glue, scissors, and modern objects to construct your scale model or collage of what you want. This makes your vision more solid and grounded in this reality — it adds concreteness to your vision.

Sam was at his wit's end. He had run ads, worked with headhunters, and interviewed dozens of prospective technicians; he had hired some, but he was way understaffed for a major project he was attempting to start up. He had venture capital funding for one year only, and without enough staff, he could never produce the unique software that had been designed — potentially a great application for millions of Internet users. At the time, the market for good technicians was tight; there were many more plum positions than well-trained experts.

Sam contacted us for some help with his situation and arranged for a consultation. When we proposed to Sam that his situation was in fact part of his deeper intention, he became furious. He was angry because he felt it was not his fault that the job market was so tight. We pointed out to him that it indeed was not his fault, because he was certainly not to blame. But, we explained, if he continued to see himself as a victim, he would not build enough power to alter his situation. Therefore, he had to shift his position to one of empowerment, to being in the driver's seat of his experience.

To do this, he had to become more neutral, and one good way to do that was to see himself as the scriptwriter of his play. In this particular scene he couldn't find the right employees. We suggested that he write a scene in which he did find them. By shifting to the position of scriptwriter, Sam could detach enough from his frustration to feel creative and excited about a possible solution.

We had him write out all his frustrations to get them out of the way. We suggested next that he build his power base by taking four days off and going to a favorite beach in Northern California. We had him state clearly what he wanted and we involved him in power path exercises to bring about the desired results. Suddenly, even though the job market remained unchanged, applications from qualified technicians increased. This first bit of success rekindled his energy, and he began to work with power path principles in earnest. Within a month his department was staffed and he was well on his way to reaching his production goal.

The four exercises that follow can all help you achieve re-intention and result in more energy and power.

Exercise 1: Successes

Write down three things that you experienced at work in the past that had satisfying results. Look to see if you believe that at some level you intended those things to happen. If you cannot see your intent in what happened, a shaman would say you are not taking responsibility for your successes; you are, rather, seeing yourself as the passive recipient of positive outcomes, as if other forces brought them about, whereas in fact your intention created them.

Exercise 2: Failures

Now write down three things that had an unfavorable outcome and look to see if you intended those things to turn out the way they did. Be careful not to become defensive or dismissive. The shaman's way is to see his or her intent in everything, good or bad. Shamans learn not to take things personally but rather to take responsibility for everything in their experience. See if you can do this with this exercise. You will know you are making progress when you can see your intention in something that is very difficult to take responsibility for — like being fired or demoted or losing a contract.

Exercise 3: How It Is

Write down what you are intending in your life right now. To do this, all you have to do is describe the way your life is, right now. Is it what you want to intend? If not, then accept your hand in it, and re-intend it in a new way. Do the exercise again one month later and compare the results.

Exercise 4: "Subconscious Dumping"

Empty your subconscious by writing down all your concerns, fears, and negative beliefs that make you feel you can't change a situation. Keep writing until you have exhausted the subject.

Another way of approaching this is to write down what you would rather see and experience, then list all the reasons you feel or believe it can't be that way. Write until you have named every possible obstacle you can think of. Do this exercise again one month later, and you'll probably find the situation has substantially improved.

SUMMARY

Important Concepts to Remember

- You can manifest power only when you focus your attention and intention in the present.
- Attention is a product of human awareness, the capacity to attend to what is going on internally and externally at all times.
- Intent directs your focus and guides your attention.

- Intention makes things happen.
- Re-intending requires first that you become neutral.
- To find this neutrality, you have to first accept things as they are now, and then to "dump" — empty out — what is in your subconscious.
- Becoming neutral and emptying your subconscious free you to build power and refocus your intention on something new.

Chapter 23

THE POWER OF SEEING

Power is the product of perception. . . . If you feel inspired by watching the sunrise, that enthusiasm you experience is the effect of power, or the effect of having perceived.

— Theun Mares, *Return of the Warriors: The Toltec Teachings*

RULE 10 CONTINUED

The smaller the degree of separation,
the greater the power available.

SEEING

For shamans, attention and intention cannot be fully exercised without the third quality that they universally call *seeing*. In fact, the word *shaman* is an ancient Siberian word meaning to see, a skill held in the highest regard by shamans the world over. By *seeing*, a shaman means using the sixth sense, going beyond what the eyes alone perceive.

In Australia, the aboriginal peoples call this ability seeing with the "strong eye," and with it they report seeing diseases in the body as if they had X-ray vision. The strong eye also refers to the ability to see events taking place at a great distance, well beyond the visual range of the eyes alone. In the West this is often referred to as remote viewing, and there has been a great amount of scientific research on it; it has been employed by the military, police, psychics, and others for years.

Without this ability to see into things or across great distances, shamans consider themselves to be handicapped; having to rely on the reports of others or on indirect means of diagnosis thus limiting a shaman's powers and effectiveness. Consequently, seeing is critical for shamans, and they train constantly to develop their ability to see, often purposely closing their eyes and practicing their inner visionary skills. Their success at this depends on how much light they access to illuminate their visions. "Seeing," when done properly, results in deep inspiration, illumination, and enlightenment, similar in nature to the experience of a scientist, scholar, or inventor who makes a great discovery. When Einstein "saw" and understood the mathematics leading to the theory of relativity, he was inspired and illuminated with his knowledge. This is not an exaggeration; if you read the writings of Einstein you discover an enlightened mind. More typically, seeing is like an inspired dream, where a direction or choice becomes clear or obvious.

The Qualities of Seeing

True seeing thus goes beyond visual perception and includes all the senses — even some senses that, according to shamans, modern scientists have not yet discerned or acknowledged. A shaman is *seeing* when able to perceive deeply what someone means, even when that person is not being obvious or when they are trying to mask what they are saying; by seeing, a shaman senses the implications of what someone is saying, even when the person is unaware of them. A good shaman can see into the subconscious. Of course, like any good psychologist or intuitive person, shamans gather this knowledge by paying close attention to such things as inflection, context, and cadence of the words as well as subtle gestures, eye movements, and postural cues. But shamanic seeing is much more than reading verbal or visual cues; seeing has more to do with a direct flow of information from one to another, made possible by aligning energy fields. While this may sound strange, it is not unlike the transmission of data to a telephone, television, or computer screen: once a number, channel, or address has been set, the information can flow through the accessed channel.

A person who sees perceives far more information than one who is not trained to see. Seeing requires skills similar to those of a tracker who, reading only faint tracks, can tell what types of animals passed by, how many were traveling and in which direction, and even their probable weight and condition. The untrained eye might miss the tracks altogether. A shaman, when meeting someone, picks up a great deal about a person using the techniques of seeing, while someone unskilled could tell very little about them, except for obvious external things like age, gender, and race.

Consider the following scenario: A prospective employee is interviewed for a position in sales at a large furniture outlet. Several different managers interview her — a well-dressed woman in her early thirties — and when they meet afterward to compare notes, they discover very different impressions.

Manager 1: "She seems professional enough, and she's aggressive. Her résumé looks good, and she had high volume in her last position. I say we give her a try."

Manager 2: "I agree that she presents herself very well and seems like just what we need, but I just wasn't comfortable with her. It's probably just a personal thing. I should give her the benefit of the doubt and vote her in."

Manager 3: "I vote no. I don't trust her a bit — I think she was lying about everything. She didn't answer one question honestly, and she's running scared. She has a good, charming cover for distracting you, but she can't be trusted and will be a disaster if we hire her."

Manager 1: "Now how did you come up with that? I think you're flat-out wrong this time. She's professional, productive, and charming. She'll be a winner for us."

Manager 3: "Well, I don't know, but I really feel something isn't right. Let's check up on her references and find out more about her before making a final decision."

Next day:

Manager 3: "Every reference she gave us was either fabricated or she lied about it in some way. I did a little checking around, and it turns out she was fired from her last job two weeks ago for embezzling funds. They're taking legal action against her. She's a nightmare candidate."

Manager 1: "I don't get it. How did you know? I didn't see it at all. She fooled me — all professional and charming, with a great looking résumé."

Manager 3: "I wasn't looking at her act and I wasn't listening to her words all that much — I was noticing how deftly she avoided answering questions that I asked and how she gave me answers she wanted me to hear. I saw that when she smiled her eyes didn't smile too. I listened for something deeper, and basically she as much as told me she was lying. I felt her deception in ways I can't even begin to describe."

Obviously, then, skills in seeing come in handy in the business world, especially when it's necessary to rapidly assess an individual or situation. Interviews with prospective employees, meetings with new clients, and even every moment of the day-to-day routine benefit greatly when you can see with greater acuity. The good news is that seeing is a trainable skill that is easily learned, not some mysterious act of sorcery, as some would believe. The truth is that seeing has many levels and the average person can learn to see much better with a little practice using exercises that, though they might at first seem a little strange, will definitely help.

Exercise 1: Stopping the World

Practice freeze-framing your experience. Take a mental snapshot of whatever is happening at any particular time during the day, and spend a few minutes examining the freeze-frame photograph, noting your thought, feeling, and perception in that moment of time. Do it without judgment. Examine the amount of information available in that freeze-frame.

What if that single moment was all you had to go on to hire someone or to decide on a project, a product, or a merger? What would it tell you? Doing this once can be eye-opening — if you do it several times a day, you will access your intuition, the source of a great amount of power.

Exercise 2: Seeing Edges

Practice seeing visually by looking at the edge of things instead of directly at them. For example, look at the outline of someone instead of looking directly. You will find that you begin to pick up different sets of information than you did before. Try not to be too demanding regarding what you see or how you receive information. This exercise, like the others, should be playful and done in a spirit of relaxation. Give it more than one try; you are not likely to get results from one attempt. Remember that experienced shamans spend many hours, days, and weeks with exercises like this one.

Exercise 3: Attending to Implications

In a conversation with another person, pay attention to the implications of the communication instead of the surface meaning. What is the person being careful not to say? Does it feel like they're avoiding something? What do you feel they're communicating behind the words, smiles, or frowns?

This is especially good to do while listening to a

politician speak because they are trained not to say what they believe or mean. Watch for visual clues. When some politicians are being interviewed on television, for example, watch to see if they rub their noses after a question; typically it means they don't like the question and are uncomfortable or feel put on the defensive by it. Watch to see whether they lie, watch to see if they act completely at ease with what they're saying, even when you know they're not. With practice you will find that you can let go of focusing on the visual cues and you'll simply know what is true and what is not.

Exercise 4: Matching Colors

Using your imagination, see, sense, or feel the color that you perceive over another person's head. This takes practice and some playfulness. If you are willing to experiment with this, you can get several people to do the same thing and then compare notes, seeing how many of you agree on the color. If you get different colors, however, it does not mean anyone is wrong; it simply means you perceive the same thing a little differently.

When you have sensed a color, then imagine a similar but slightly different color over your own head. Try talking to the person under these conditions. Can you sense a difference between this "color-enhanced" conversation and an ordinary one? With practice, the matching color technique can bring you into a much greater state of communication: you will perceive more about the person than you ordinarily would.

SUMMARY

Important Concepts to Remember

- For shamans, attention and intention cannot be fully exercised without the third quality of *seeing*.
- By *seeing*, a shaman means seeing using the sixth sense, going beyond what the eyes alone perceive.
- True seeing goes beyond visual perception and includes all the senses.
- Seeing means sensing the implications of what someone is saying even when they themselves are unaware of them.
- Seeing is more than reading verbal or visual cues; seeing has more to do with a direct flow of information from one to another, made possible by aligning energy fields.
- Seeing has many levels, and with a little practice, the average person can learn to see much better. This is a gateway into the intuition, into the source of a great amount of power.

Chapter 24

STALKING THE PREY

Warriors make an inventory of energy expenditures. That allows them to know through the technique of stalking, how they use their energy and later to plan a strategy for redirecting its use; thereby they increase their available energy.

— Victor Sanchez, *The Teachings of Don Carlos*

RULE 6 CONTINUED

Power can be hunted and gained in ways similar to the rules of the hunt in the natural environment.

We have seen that the source of our power is within. We have done various exercises and had a few moments of awakening, and we have realized that certain things we do develop a great amount of power. These include discovering powerful places in nature; being with powerful people; practicing clear communication and truthfulness; maintaining silence; practicing power gathering exercises such as chi kung and t'ai chi; developing clear intent; creating strong mental focus and imagination; being adaptable and flexible; observing gratitude; developing harmony between masculine and feminine sides; and being of service. We have also seen that certain behaviors result in a loss of power. It is very good to ask, then, what we can do to avoid the behavior that causes a weakening of power? Shamans over many centuries have developed methods for getting rid of fruitless ways of thinking and unproductive actions. They simply apply what they know best from their outdoor lives to the elimination of power leaks. A shaman stalks behaviors and attitudes that cause power loss just as a hunter or predator hunts prey. We have observed that when one stalks and eliminates power leaks they automatically become more powerful. Hunting for the power leaks results in an overall power gain just as when a predator stalks the weaknesses of the herd, they become more powerful by having a meal. Here's how it works.

Stalking

Humans are natural predators and hunters — and we can apply the principles of hunting to effectively eliminate unwanted behaviors and attitudes in ourselves. Stalking involves closely observing, without judgment, certain habits and recurrent patterns of behavior and thinking. Just as an animal becomes prey when it is caught by its own habitual patterns or predictable behavior, the more predictable your routines are, the more a victim you become and the less power you have.

The successful predator devotes time to patiently watching its prey, studying its habits and movements. Careful observation of your behavior and thinking will help you remove the obstacles to preserving and building your power.

Look at a mountain lion stalking its prey, for example. A lion is willing to spend many hours watching, observing, and studying the habits of its prey. It makes no move, but simply stores its power and waits for the proper moment to spring. For the lion or any predator, a successful hunt depends upon exact timing. When the time has come for action, the lion puts everything into its charge. There is no hesitation, no ambivalence, no holding back. This strategy results in a meal more often then not. When the lion fails, it merely tries again.

Predators and Prey

Shamans suggest we take a good look at the dance between predator and prey, and see the significant difference between them. First of all, predators stalk, prey do not. Successful predators are less predictable in their behavior; they are more spontaneous, flexible, and adaptable to many conditions. Prey, on the other hand, tend to follow predictable routines. A prairie dog, for example, will not come out of its hole until the air has reached a certain temperature. Its predator the hawk waits for the temperature to rise, which also helps it to attain loft, and when the prairie dog predictably pops out of its burrow, the hawk has lunch.

Human beings, with their simian bodies and large brains, are natural predators. Shamans in particular, armed with knowledge from the natural environment, understand and use this natural instinct to their advantage. Most important of all, they apply the rules of predation to what they call the parasites within. They become predators to all the negative behaviors and ways of thinking that create power loss. These negative behaviors and patterns of thinking, the shaman's prey, fall into seven primary groupings.

The Seven Types of Prey

1. Self-destructive behavior
2. Greed
3. Self-deprecation
4. Arrogance
5. Impatience
6. Victimization or martyrdom
7. Stubbornness

1. Self-Destructive Behavior

This is the first obvious behavior to look for — to stalk and hunt and eliminate. Self-destructive behavior shows itself in addictions, erratic behavior, violence, abuse, reckless driving, drugs, criminal activity. These signs are obvious when we look for them.

2. Greed

This behavior is based on fear — a fear of lack, of scarcity — and results in overconsumption of food or drink, hoarding, grabbing, stealing, depriving others, selfishness, using people, or cheating.

3. Self-Deprecation

This is based on a fear of inadequacy and results in self put-downs, fear of trying, lack of assertiveness, excessive apologizing, being "invisible," shallow breathing, underestimating one's abilities, depression, and unwillingness to make the best effort.

4. Arrogance

Arrogance or self-importance is based on a fear of being vulnerable; it leads to hiding mistakes, bragging, keeping others away, avoiding intimacy, overestimating one's abilities, inability to apologize, inflating, exaggerating, excessive attention on self, sense of superiority, and wanting special treatment.

5. Impatience

Impatience is based on a fear of running out of time; this fear — like so many others — has a fear of scarcity at its core. Impatience reveals itself in rushing, always being late, interrupting, being intolerant or impulsive, running over others, being accident prone, being distracted, being full of expectations, forcing, living in chaos and disorganization, being unwilling to wait and observe.

6. Victimization or martyrdom

Victimization or martyrdom comes from a fear of being trapped by people or circumstances; underneath is a deep fear of powerlessness. It results in whining, misdirected complaining, resentment, assigning blame, backbiting, vengeance, argumentativeness, self-pity, disrespect for boundaries, emotional suffering, and a failure to take responsibility.

7. Stubbornness

This destructive form of behavior is based on a fear of losing independence, or fear of loss or change. It is marked by inflexibility, inattentiveness, being stuck in the past, argumentativeness, resistance, sullenness, aloofness, passive aggressiveness, and rigidity.

These seven types of negative behavior and thinking are responsible for almost all losses of personal power, and shamans therefore make a point of closely observing and eliminating them.*

SUMMARY

Important Concepts to Remember

- Over the course of centuries, shamans have perfected a powerful method for getting rid of unproductive actions and fruitless ways of thinking.

---

* To learn more about these seven patterns, see *Transforming Your Dragons* by José Stevens (Sante Fe, NM: Bear and Company, 1994).

- Stalking involves closely observing, without judgment, certain recurrent patterns of behavior and thinking.
- Shamans recommend becoming more predatory. Predators stalk, prey do not.
- Successful predators tend to be less predictable in behavior than their prey — they are more spontaneous, flexible, and adaptive to many conditions.
- A shaman stalks behaviors and attitudes that cause power loss just as a hunter or predator seeks prey.
- There are seven types of prey:

  1. Self-destructive behavior
  2. Greed
  3. Self-deprecation
  4. Arrogance
  5. Impatience
  6. Victimization
  7. Stubbornness

Chapter 25

REQUIREMENTS OF A SUCCESSFUL STALKER

In learning to break free of social conditioning, an apprentice must learn to stalk both himself and those around him. . . . No true warrior who walks the path of freedom will ever use stalking to force another being into doing his bidding. Never!

— Theun Mares, *Return of the Warriors: The Toltec Teachings*

RULE 6 CONTINUED

Power can be hunted and gained in ways similar to the rules of the hunt in the natural environment.

The shamans we studied with had carefully analyzed the requirements of a successful tracker or stalker and categorized these requirements so that we could not only study them, but implement them in our lives.

There are seven requirements of the successful stalker:

1. Have no self-pity.
2. Use your intuition 100 percent.
3. Be patient.
4. Be humble.
5. Assume nothing.
6. Take full responsibility.
7. Be ruthlessly unattached.

1. Have No Self-Pity

You cannot be a successful stalker if you indulge in feeling sorry for yourself. Self-pity is also a form of self-importance, which a stalker can ill afford. Power comes from eliminating self-importance and self-pity.

Translation to Business

The business world can be a ruthless competitive jungle with ample opportunities for self-pity. But you can choose, instead, to focus on your allies, the extraordinarily helpful people who want you to succeed, and the options that allow you to survive and thrive in the face of strong obstacles. You can choose to focus on the half of the glass that is full — your strengths — rather than the empty half — your weaknesses and problems.

Faced with a demotion, a possible pay cut, or loss of

a project, a master shaman would waste no time in self-pity but would immediately look at possible strategies and available options that can turn the situation of a potential power loss into one of a power gain.

2. Use Your Intuition 100 Percent

A successful tracker can go beyond intellect and reasoning and access intuition. Intuition is knowing what is beyond rationality and is accessed through the second attention, through an awareness of your inner feelings. It is a source of great power, for it clearly shows you what should be done and when. If you doubt your intuition and refuse to act from it, you will never be very powerful.

Translation to Business

Any CEO worth their paycheck knows the advantages and the power of using intuition because it has always been an essential ingredient to a company's successful founding and ongoing success. Logic, number crunching, and bottom-line reasoning are common in most organization — and they are essential as well — but the person who goes with intuition when faced with a tough decision can be a rare and valuable boon to any organization.

A successful manufacturer of electric heaters had the opportunity to widen its product line to include electric water pumps by purchasing an undercapitalized company that had stumbled in the marketplace. The

number crunchers were thumbs down on the deal but
the CEO of the heater company couldn't shut out the
inner voice that told him to buy the pump company.
After consulting with everyone and considering the deal
very carefully, he proceeded to purchase the company
after striking a deal with very favorable terms. To everyone's surprise the pump division broke even in the first
six months and in a year's time was turning a 20 percent profit. If the rational reasoning of the accountants
and lawyers had been valued 20 percent more than intuition, the CEO would never have made the deal and lost
the opportunity to expand the power of many individuals in that organization.

3. Be Patient

To those who are patient and willing to wait for the
proper moment go the spoils. Patience is the hunter's
best friend. It rewards the hunter by revealing the perfect time to act — and timing is everything.

Translation to Business

Angelina, an up-and-coming fashion designer,
worked long and passionately for months on a line of
winter clothes for an upscale clothing manufacturer.
The firm wanted to unveil the line in the summer to
take advantage of an early start. Although she was
essentially finished with the project, she felt strongly
that her line would be lost in the flood of other fashions
hitting the market at the same time. She managed to
convince the manufacturer to wait several weeks before

unveiling her new line, giving her greater access to media coverage and advertising markets. The ploy proved extremely successful and the line opened to a very receptive marketplace and tremendous sales. This is a good example of the powerful contribution of intuition and patience.

4. Have Humility

Humility is not self-deprecating — it is wonderfully freeing instead. To be humble is to laugh at yourself, no matter what has happened, whether you've failed or won. Humility attacks a hunter's greatest enemy — the specter of self-importance. In a shaman's frame of reference, humility is not self-conscious modesty or groveling, rather it is being unattached to the desire to be the center of attention, to have the ego massaged, or to be publicly praised. Humility means realizing that you could just as well have failed; it means being grateful to spirit and to those who made your success possible.

Translation to Business

Brad was the most consistent and successful salesperson in his real estate office. For five years running he had won the sales award from the division and was regularly among the top three salespeople of the month for his company throughout the entire state. Although he was exceptionally successful, he regularly referred clients to colleagues and went out of his way to help his sales team when a deal threatened to fall apart. He became known as the "saver," because he worked like the saving pitcher in baseball. He was known for his great sense of humor and never took himself too seriously, win or lose. He never failed to pay generous referral fees and always went out of his way to acknowledge any help he received, from the receptionist on up to the legal team. Although he was a great success and had a lot to be proud of, he still had humility — little or no ego to get in the way. As a result, people would make every effort to help him, and they all became more powerful, more successful, in the process.

5. Make No Assumptions

For a stalker, each situation is brand new. Each event must be approached afresh, and then nothing, not the slightest detail, will be missed. This rabbit is different from the last rabbit — perhaps it is larger or faster, perhaps the heat of the day stronger or the terrain more difficult. Nothing can be taken for granted, nothing assumed in the hunt. In this way the tracker prevails and the hunt is successful.

Translation to Business

When a major motion picture studio lost out on an attempt to purchase a successful smaller studio, the president of the larger studio went on a fact-finding mission. After interviewing the key players, he determined that the source of their failure was the complacency of the team and the assumptions they made about the finality of the deal. Since the studio had successfully acquired several companies in the past, they had approached this potential acquisition as if it were a done deal. They lacked enthusiasm for purchasing the new studio, acted arrogantly at meetings, and made it seem like they were doing the small studio a favor. Much to the shock of the major studio, the deal fell through, not because they could not agree on a purchase price but simply because the smaller studio didn't like the way they were treated. They sold to a rival studio for an equal amount.

6. Take Full Responsibility

For the master hunter there can be no one — or thing — to blame for failure. Blame and finger pointing are a waste of precious energy and power and cannot be indulged in. This includes blaming yourself. For a stalker, blame is irrelevant, and taking full responsibility is essential. Taking responsibility means realizing that the success of the hunt lies totally on making the most of one's skills, knowledge, and power to ensure a successful hunt.

Translation to Business

The Japanese have a saying, "Fix the problem, not the blame." This is the shamanic viewpoint as well. Hunting for the culprit and fixing blame is a favorite game, but it's a completely fruitless and destructive one.

An example: A legal firm missed an important

filing deadline that reduced the value of a case by several million dollars. They went on a witch-hunt to find the responsible individual. When they found the legal assistant who should have filed the document, she was fired on the spot, even though several lawyers gave her contradictory information about the filing deadline. The firm believed that this would send a message to the rest of the team not to make a similar mistake — but, instead, failures to file happened several times in the course of the next six months. Each time, someone was blamed and fired with great fanfare. But then suddenly the firm had a new problem. It suffered an exodus of paralegals and legal assistants and could not hire anyone to replace them because word had gotten out; no one wanted to work in such a stressful environment despite its high pay. Some timely consultation revealed that the problem had less to do with individual failure and much to do with the firm's communication system and confusing way of handling cases. They initiated a team approach along with a new calendar system, and the problem of missed deadlines disappeared.

7. Be Detached

A stalker cannot afford to be sentimental. When a stalker observes that a particular attitude, action, or behavior causes a power loss, it is ruthlessly cut out. There can be no attachment to the behavior. If attachment to an emotion or idea results in a loss of power, a shaman detaches from that behavior and eliminates it, no matter how much gratification might be derived from it, no matter how much fear arises with leaving it behind.

Translation to Business

A large commercial wholesaler selling directly to the public received a series of complaints from its female employees regarding sexual harassment at one of its locations. When investigators looked into the matter, apparently the alleged harassment had been going on for months and the complaints lodged with the foreman had been largely ignored. Eventually the employees had gone over his head and complained to headquarters directly. Investigators turned up over one hundred incidents of blatant sexual harassment during the past year.

When the foreman was interviewed, he smiled at the male interviewer and said it was a guy thing and the women were acting provocatively anyway. He was hoping that, since the investigator was male, they would establish a bond and that would be the end of the matter. His effort failed and he was terminated within the week, along with two other male employees who had been responsible for the harassment. The company managed to avert a major lawsuit.

The company showed a good degree of detachment throughout the process: They discovered the attitudes and actions that were causing the power loss, and they got rid of the people causing it.

SUMMARY

Important Concepts to Remember

- According to shamans, there are seven requirements of the successful tracker or stalker:

    1. Have no self pity.
    2. Use your intuition 100 percent.
    3. Be patient.
    4. Have humility (be able to laugh at yourself).
    5. Make no assumptions.
    6. Take full responsibility.
    7. Be detached.

Chapter 26

THE PRIMARY PRINCIPLES OF STALKING

Without the concerted effort to track down and eliminate your foibles, and to recognize and bolster your strengths, you lose sight of the principal purpose of tracking: the pursuit of freedom.

— Ken Eagle Feather, *A Toltec Path*

RULE 6 CONTINUED

Power can be hunted and gained in ways similar to the rules of the hunt in the natural environment.

We have just seen the seven requirements for successful stalking. As you work to fulfill them, keep these principles in mind:

1. Choose your hunting ground.
2. Eliminate the nonessentials.
3. Consider every battle a life-and-death struggle.
4. Observe, observe, observe.
5. Integrate.
6. Attack with lightning speed.
7. Give absolute power and energy.
8. If at first you don't succeed, relax!

Let's examine each of these eight principles.

1. Choose Your Hunting Ground

Only a fool tries to hunt in any situation. You must choose where and when to strike. The wise stalker chooses her hunting ground, where and when to strike; if you allow your prey to dictate the battlefield, it will most likely win and you will lose.

Translation to Business

A computer software company hired a business consultant in high demand to help them make some hard decisions about product line and break through an impasse in sales. The consultant proposed that she tour their site, but when they asked her to provide consultation in their offices, she politely declined. She proposed that she and the senior vice president meet at an out-of-the-way bookstore with an adjacent coffee shop at a time when the place would be practically empty. At first the company balked, but they eventually agreed to the location, and as it turned out, they had several very productive talks there.

The consultant knew that meeting at the company site, with its problematic atmosphere of feeling stuck, would likely produce more of the same feeling. She knew she needed to get the senior vice president out of his environment and into a place that was both neutral and promotive of fresh ideas. The bookstore was just the place.

2. Eliminate the Nonessentials

Most problems are problems because there are so many tangled elements intertwined that the situation is difficult to understand. It's a little like looking into a drawer for a pen and seeing such a mess that you want to just close it and give up the search. The key is to eliminate everything that does not apply to the immediate situation — eliminate everything that is not a pen.

The stalking lion eliminates everything from its attention that is not essential to the capture of its prey. Other animals may be milling around even closer than the target animal, but when the lion zeros in on the lame gazelle, it ignores all other animals. Success of the hunt depends on concentration on the target and elimination of all nonessentials.

Translation to Business

A consultant was called into a pharmaceutical firm to get to the source of low morale and staff discontent.

She interviewed mid-level managers, support staff, and top management and heard many contradictory stories about who was at fault. Mid-level management blamed top management for decisions that contributed to low morale. Top management blamed incompetence on the part of support staff. Support staff suggested that mid-level managers didn't fight hard enough for their well-being, preferring to play it safe instead. All the contradictory information could have been totally confusing to anyone who was trying to assign blame for the problem. However the consultant was trained in system's approach and so she discarded any information that led to blame or attack. Instead she looked at processes that undermined authority or that contributed to poor communication. By focusing on these weaknesses and refusing to be distracted, she came up with five proposals to correct the problems in morale. Among several procedural changes, she implemented a system where top management met with support staff once a month to hear their grievances and their suggestions for improvements in production, sales, and marketing. Without anyone losing their job, morale improved dramatically over the next several months.

3. Consider Every Battle a Life and Death Struggle

This principle focuses on commitment and determination. When your life is at stake, you make an absolute commitment of all your power to your survival.

For a shaman, the proper way to approach every task is with absolute commitment. The shaman realizes that a predator is not automatically successful because it is equipped with sharper teeth or stronger muscles. A predator can be seriously injured or even killed during the hunt. The lion kicked in the jaw by a zebra might be unable to hunt and die of starvation. So, in every hunt, the hunter must be prepared to die. But this threat gives the hunter an advantage because it ensures that they will operate at peak performance level, completely at attention, keenly observant of everything in their environment, and fully in charge at the moment of action.

Translation to Business

The lead lawyer in a medical malpractice suit instructed an assistant attorney to research a remote cause of disability that seemed to be completely unrelated to the injury of the plaintiff. The assistant wondered why she was asked to pursue such an arcane matter, considering they had compiled an ironclad case against the defendant. The lead lawyer carefully explained, "When I'm in that courtroom, I don't want to be blindsided by even a remote argument claiming the injury was caused by something we haven't researched. I've seen strong cases go down just because one remote possibility wasn't considered. I want not only a preponderance of evidence, I want every possible avenue of escape shut down." This is the response of a successful hunter.

4. Observe, Observe, Observe

The hunter lurks, watching every move, every small behavior of its prey. The hunter observes that its prey routinely gathers at a certain spot at the same time every day and notices a weakness or vulnerability in the herd. The hunter observes the one old antelope that tends to lag behind the others or the calf that strays from its mother's side, and then moves in for the successful kill. The wise hunter notices the strengths and weaknesses of its prey. A cheetah will not attack a calf encircled by a group of mature water buffalo.

Translation to Business

The president and owner of a brokerage firm in New York was considering entering into a partnership with a broker in Chicago, an agreement that would involve a considerable amount of money. They had some good meetings that seemed to go well and a contract was imminent, but the New York broker had some reservations.

We suggested that rather than be too eager to sign, he sit back and observe his prospective partner — and himself as well — when they were together. During their next meeting he observed the Chicago broker take a call from one of his assistants and noticed how badly the broker treated his employee on the phone. He also noticed how badly he himself felt as a result of overhearing the call. By the end of their fourth meeting, the New York broker had made a number of observations that convinced him the partnership would come to grief one way or another. In the end, he didn't sign the contract and likely saved himself serious trouble.

5. Integrate

After carefully observing for minutes, perhaps even hours without moving a muscle, the lion senses that the time is right for the charge. This moment of integration is very brief but extraordinarily complex and important to the success of the overall hunt. In this moment of perception, the hunter goes deep within to integrate all the observations and stored calculations obtained so painstakingly during the long wait. The lion engages in innumerable calculations that include its own bodily functions, wind speed, outside temperature, current distance to the prey, size, weight and condition of the prey, impact speed and probable location of impact, possible obstacles in the environment, and countless other variables. This rapid integral assessment is so deep that it bypasses conscious awareness, resulting in the appearance that the lion is doing nothing at all but crouching with intensity and anticipation. Without this powerful integration, all the observation is for naught. Integration is the moment when everything comes together in a laserlike focus.

Translation to Business

A genetic research company had been engaged for several years on a project to grow replacement human body parts from animal tissue. During this time, based on extensive research, many experiments, and observing many outcomes, the staff developed two distinct approaches to growing the tissue. Both methods were viable and each had pros and cons that made a choice between them difficult. Each team of researchers responsible for developing the two methods presented their cases to the team of four partners, the scientists who owned the corporation. After the presentations, the partners thanked the teams and then met to finalize the choice of which method they were going to pursue. After hours of discussion and poring over the results of the research, they decided to take a break. None of them had reached a final conclusion. Accustomed to the process of making hard decisions, they all agreed that during their break they would rest from any more document reading and try to get away from it all. One of the partners went for a long walk on the beach near their facility and another chose to nap for a couple of hours. A third partner climbed on his bicycle and went for a ride while the fourth took time to do his t'ai chi and yoga routines in the gym. When they all gathered together again, each had finalized a choice. Each of them, in their own way, had gone deeply into an integrative state and somehow, everything they had been exposed to had come together into a clear perception of what should be done. All of them had reached the same conclusion and they made the choice easily without conflict or wrangling.

6. Attack with Lightning Speed

A falcon doesn't stop mid-flight to think about whether to go for the gray squirrel or to wait for a more attractive red one, nor does it float lazily down to grab its prey. The falcon dives with maximum speed to grab its targeted prey. The successful hunter attacks suddenly, decisively, and with maximum force. There is usually no second chance; a lightning response is critical. Note that quick action in this case is not haste that comes from impatience — it is timeliness based on knowledge, experience, and careful calculation.

Translation to Business

Robert, a senior vice president of a computer firm, received a call from his old college buddy, Tim. His friend had just succeeded in producing a highly specialized security software program for a rival company and then taken a month off for rest and relaxation. Now he was looking for a new project. Robert knew that in the high-octane environment of the computer world, experts in security systems are gobbled up immediately because of the high demand for their skills; he also knew that normal hiring procedures demanded sets of interviews with senior staff and that Tim would be long gone if made to follow protocol. Robert calculated that Tim would be a huge asset to the firm, considered the situation, and offered him a job on the spot, even before he called the president to get his approval. He reached the president within the hour, secured his approval, and sealed the deal that afternoon. He acted with speed, when the time felt right, even though it involved personal risk.

7. Give Absolute Power and Energy

Speed is not enough to secure prey. Along with speed, the hunter must have enough power and mass to take down prey. A fox can't bring down an antelope nor can an eagle pick up an elk, though each is a highly skilled hunter capable of handling sizeable prey when they use maximum power and energy. The cheetah has the speed to catch an antelope, but if it is too exhausted from the chase, it might not bring the antelope down or fend off competing predators.

Translation to Business

A media company's Internet division was growing by leaps and bounds. When reports suggested the Christmas holidays would bring a boom in product sales, the warehouse went to double shifts and hired 25 percent more staff in October. By holiday time they fulfilled all the orders on time without resorting to troublesome back ordering.

8. If at First You Don't Succeed, Relax!

The secret to surviving in the rough-and-tumble world of the hunt is to conserve energy whenever you are not engaged in an all-out attack. Think of the cat on its side lazily licking its fur as if it hadn't a care in the world; rather than pacing in anxiety or frustration after an intense but failed chase, the cat rests to regain strength and energy.

Translation to Business

When a Japanese electronics company suffered a major setback in the marketplace and was forced into bankruptcy, the chairman of the board went into his office and committed suicide. From a shamanic perspective, his response to the problem, while traditionally considered to be an honorable one, did not leave him with any other options that could have eventually led to success. Because of his choice, he not only lost the battle but also made it impossible to fight on another day. The shamanic way is to be flexible like the martial artist. Should you fail one day, you don't reproach or blame yourself; you simply observe what went wrong, learn from it, and apply the lesson to the next battle.

A skydiving instructor's chute did not open after he had jumped from a plane at a high altitude. His back-up chute failed to open as well. As he saw his death approaching, he decided to completely let go; he relaxed and allowed himself to fall to what he assumed was certain death. Instead, he landed in some trees that broke his fall. Although seriously injured, he lived to jump another day. As he told the story, he observed that his letting go saved his life. If he had hit the trees in a state of rigidity, he would certainly have been killed. Relaxing and letting go preserved him.

This principle has another important business

application as well: When you relax, you rejuvenate your energy; when you're in a stressful state, you deplete your energy. Too much stress results in a loss of power.

SUMMARY

Important Concepts to Remember

- From a shamanic perspective, there are eight primary principles of stalking or tracking:

  1. Choose your hunting ground.
  2. Eliminate the nonessentials.
  3. Consider every battle a life and death struggle.
  4. Observe, observe, observe.
  5. Integrate.
  6. Attack with lightning speed.
  7. Give absolute power and energy.
  8. If at first you don't succeed, relax!

Conclusion

I n this book we have introduced you to some basic concepts about shamanism, and we have done our best to make clear and available its extraordinary store of knowledge for leaders in the world of business and organizations.

In presenting this information we are taking a risk that some who read this material will not understand the full implications of accumulating, conserving, and directing power. Because of its potential for abuse, shamanic knowledge has been carefully guarded over the centuries and not made available to the general public. Although the potential for abuse is enormous, we believe that life is self-correcting: When someone uses power improperly, the universe, like a loving but harsh teacher, provides consequences that are painful but very effective in restoring balance in the long run. Eventually everyone learns what they can handle and what they had better not do. In the meantime, of course, some people get hurt, but that is the nature of life on this planet. We learn by experience.

Many indigenous teachers have told us that now is the time for this kind of knowledge to be made available and that it is not only good but also necessary that we write about this subject. We know that there is nothing inherently evil about doing business, as many people have come to believe. Business is nothing more than a vehicle of human exchange. The way business is conducted, however, can be shortsighted and completely reprehensible, damaging to people and the environment, and it is this that we would like to alter.

We have seen many fine and even wonderful people who earn their living doing business with others. In addition, more and more corporations are striving to genuinely help people and to bring balance back to this planet, and they are making a real contribution. The obstacles they face in a world gone astray are formidable, but they are gaining momentum every day, and they will prevail.

As a species, we have arrived at a long-prophesied point of choice that is marked by great polarization. We either join those forces that use power for the good of everyone and for harmony on this planet or we choose to go with the forces of greed, selfishness, and ultimate destruction. Increasingly, there will be no middle ground to cling to. We are choosing to throw our support toward the forces with heart, the people and organizations moving toward mutual cooperation, communication, planetary awareness, and connection with spirit in nature.

We have been taught that when individuals act with integrity and impeccability, the organizations they build will project those same values. When individuals fail to act with heart, the organizations they create will reflect extraordinary selfishness. In the short run, they may even seem to have the advantage as they prey on people's fear and align themselves with spineless politicians to create a fertile climate for more profitability based on unsustainable planetary practices. This state of affairs, however, also provides great opportunities on the path with heart. For one, it can wake people from their trancelike slumber and make them realize freedom is slipping away. Facing a formidable foe makes people strong and builds character. The ancient Chinese sages believed one should never have it too easy or the likelihood is to grow soft and weak. We need some adversity to make us strong. Fortunately there are ample petty tyrants and formidable foes to go around at this time. We either grow strong and intend a better way or we wither and die through our own ignorance.

The wisdom and expertise of indigenous peoples throughout the world can help us regain the balance required for a sustainable future. This does not mean turning back the clock — in any way. It means that, in the face of great challenges, we can, through extreme challenge, forge a new and fulfilling future using the tools we already have.

Bibliography

Shaman, Taoist, and Related

Arrien, Angeles. *The Fourfold Way: Walking the Paths of the Warrior, Teacher, Healer, Visionary*. New York: HarperCollins, 1993.

Avila, Elena. *Woman Who Glows in the Dark: A Curandera Reveals Traditional Secrets of Physical and Spiritual Health*. New York: Tarcher/Putnam, 2000.

Bear, Jaya. *Amazon Magic: The Life Story of Ayahuasquero and Shaman, Don Agustin Rivas Vasguez*. Taos, N. Mex.: Colibri Publishing, 2000.

Braden, Gregg. *Walking between the Worlds: The Science of Compassion*. Bellevue, Wash.: Radio bookstore Press, 1997.

Brown, Tom. *The Journey*. New York: Berkley Books, 1992.

Bynum, Edward. *The African Unconscious: Roots of Ancient Mysticism and Modern Psychology*. New York: Columbia University/Teacher's College Press, 1999.

Calvo, Cesar. *The Three Halves of Ino Moxo: Teachings of the Wizard of the Upper Amazon*. Translated by Ken Symington Cesar. Rochester, Vt.: Inner Traditions International, 1995.

Casteneda, Carlos. *The Teachings of Don Juan: A Yagui Way of Knowledge*. New York: Ballantine Books, 1968.

————. *A Separate Reality: Further Conversations with Don Juan*. New York: Simon and Schuster, 1971.

————. *Journey to Ixtlan: The Lessons of Don Juan*. New York: Simon and Schuster, 1972.

————. *Tales of Power*. New York: Simon and Schuster, 1974.

————. *The Eagles Gift*. New York: Simon and Schuster, 1981.

————. *The Fire from Within*. New York, Simon and Schuster, 1984.

————. *The Power of Silence: Further Lessons of Don Juan*. New York: Simon and Schuster, 1987.

————. *The Art of Dreaming*. New York: HarperCollins, 1993.

————. *Magical Passes: The Practical Wisdom of the Shamans of Ancient Mexico*. New York: HarperCollins, 1998.

————. *The Active Side of Infinity: The Practical Wisdom of the Shamans of Ancient Mexico*. New York: Harper Collins, 1998.

————. *The Wheel of Time: The Shamans of Ancient Mexico, Their Thoughts about Life, Death and the Universe*. New York: Washington Square Press, 1998.

Chatwin, Bruce. *The Songlines*. New York: Penguin Books, 1987.

Chopra, Deepak. *Creating Affluence: Wealth Consciousness in the Field of all Possibilities*. Novato, Calif.: Amber Allen/New World Library, 1992.

Cook, Pat. *Shaman, Jhankri, and Nele: Music Healers of Indigenous Cultures*. Roslyn, N.Y.: Ellipsis Arts, 1997.

Dobkin De Rios, Marlene. *Amazon Healer: The Life and Times of an Urban Shaman*. Fullerton, Calif.: California State University Fullerton, 1992.

Donner, Florinda. *Being-In-Dreaming: An Initiation into the Sorcerer's World*. N.Y.: HarperCollins, 1991.

Eagle Feather, Ken. *A Toltec Path*. Charlottesville, Va.: Hampton Roads, 1995.

Eaton, Evelyn. *The Shaman and the Medicine Wheel*. Wheaton, Ill.: The Theosophical Publishing House, 1982.

Eliade, Mircea. *Shamanism: Archaic Techniques of Ecstasy*. Princeton, N.J.: Princeton University Press, 1964.

Elkin, A. P. *Aboriginal Men of High Degree: Initiation and Sorcery in the World's Oldest Tradition*. Rochester, Vt.: Inner Traditions, 1994.

Forest, Ohky Simone. *Dreaming the Council Ways: True Native Teachings from the Red Lodge*. York Beach, Maine: Samuel Weiser, 2000.

Grim, John. *The Shaman: Patterns of Religious Healing Among the Ojibway Indians*. Norman, Okla.: University of Oklahoma Press, 1983.

Halifax, Joan. *Shamanic Voices: A Survey of Visionary Narratives*. New York: E.P. Dutton, 1979.

Harner, Michael. *The Way of the Shaman: A Guide to Power and Healing*. New York: HarperCollins, 1980.

Ingerman, Sandra. *Soul Retrieval: Mending the Fragmented Self*. New York: HarperCollins, 1991.

———. *Medicine for the Earth: How to Transform Personal and Environmental Toxins*. New York: Three Press, 2000.

Jenkins, Elizabeth. *Initiation: A Woman's Spiritual Adventure in the Heart of the Andes*. New York: G.P. Putnam's Sons, 1997.

Jones, Blackwolf. *Listen to the Drum: Blackwolf Shares His Medicine*. Center City, Minn.: Hazelden, 1995.

Kakar, Sudhir. *Shamans, Mystics, and Doctors: A Psychological Inquiry into India and its Healing Traditions*. Boston: Beacon Press, 1982.

Kharitidi, Olga. *Entering the Circle*. Albuquerque, N. Mex.: Gloria Press, 1995.

Kim, Tae-Yun. *Seven Steps to Inner Power*. Novato, Calif.: New World Library, 1991.

———. *The Silent Master: Awakening the Power Within*. Novato, Calif.: New World Library, 1994.

Lamb, F. Bruce. *Rio Tigre and Beyond*. Berkeley, Calif.: North Atlantic Books, 1985.

Larsen, Stephen. *The Shaman's Doorway*. San Francisco: HarperCollins, 1976.

Mares, Theun. *Return of the Warriors: The Toltec Teachings – Volume One: Revealing the Ancient Mystery of Atl. A Path of Freedom, Joy, and Power*. Atlanta, Ga.: LionHeart Publishing, 1995.

Mathews, John. *The Celtic Shaman: A Handbook*. Rockport, Mass.: Element Books, 1992.

Mindell, Arnold. *The Shaman's Body: A New Shamanism for Transforming Health, Relationships, and the Community*. New York: HarperCollins, 1993.

Ming-Dao, Deng. *Scholar Warrior: An Introduction to the Tao in Everyday Life*. New York: HarperCollins, 1990.

———. *Everyday Tao: Living with Balance and Harmony*. New York: HarperCollins, 1996.

Narby, Jeremy. *The Cosmic Serpent: DNA and the Origins of Knowledge*. New York: Tarcher, 1998.

Narby, Jeremy and Francis Huxley, eds. *Shamans Through Time: 500 Years on the Path to Knowledge*. New York: Tarcher/Putnam, 2001.

Nelson, Mary. *Beyond Fear: A Toltec Guide to Freedom and Joy*. San Francisco: Council Oak Books, 1997.

Nicholson, Shirley. *Shamanism*. Wheaton, Ill.: The Theosophical
Publishing House, 1987.

Nowak, Margaret and Stephen Durrant. *The Tale of a Nisan Shamaness:
A Manchu Folk Epic*. Seattle: University of Washington Press, 1977.

Orieax, Jean. *Talleyrand: The Art of Survival*. Translated by Patricia
Wolf. New York: Knopf, 1974.

Parker, K. Langloh. *Wise Women of the Dreamtime*. Rochester, Vt.: Inner
Traditions International, 1993.

Perkins, John. *The World as You Dream It: Shamanic Teachings from the
Amazon and Andes*. Rochester, Vt.: Destiny Books, 1994.

Perry, Forest. *The Violet Forest: Shamanic Journeys in the Amazon*. Santa
Fe, N. Mex.: Bear and Company, 1998.

Pinkson, Tom Soloway. *The Flowers of Wiricuta: A Journey to Shamanic
Power with the Huichol Indians of Mexico*. Rochester, Vt.: Destiny
Books, 1995.

Proceedings of the Third International Conference on the Study of
Shamanism and Alternate Modes of Healing. Berkeley, Calif.:
Independent Scholars of Asia, Inc. 1986.

Proceedings of the Fourth International Conference on the Study of
Shamanism and Alternate Modes of Healing. Berkeley, Calif.:
Independent Scholars of Asia, Inc. 1987.

Proceedings of the Fifth International Conference on the Study of
Shamanism and Alternate Modes of Healing. Berkeley, Calif.:
Independent Scholars of Asia, Inc. 1988.

Proceedings of the Sixth International Conference on the Study of
Shamanism and Alternate Modes of Healing. Berkeley, Calif.:
Independent Scholars of Asia, Inc. 1989.

Proceedings of the Seventh International Conference on the Study of
Shamanism and Alternate Modes of Healing. Berkeley, Calif.:
Independent Scholars of Asia, Inc. 1990.

Reinhard, Johan. *Machu Pichu: The Sacred Center*. Lima, Peru: Nuevas
Imagenes, 1991.

Roads, Michael J. *Talking with Nature*. Tiburon, Calif.: H.J. Kramer Inc. 1985.

Ruiz, Miguel. *The Mastery of Love: A Practical Guide to the Art of
Relationship*. San Rafael, Calif.: Amber-Allen Publishing, 1997.

———. *The Four Agreements: A Practical Guide to Personal Freedom*. San
Rafael, Calif.: Amber-Allen Publishing, 1999.

Sanchez, Victor. *The Teachings of Don Carlos: Practical Applications of
the Works of Carlos Casteneda*. Translated by Robert Nelson. Santa
Fe, N. Mex.: Bear and Company, 1995.

———. *Toltecs of the New Millenium*. Translated by Robert Nelson.
Santa Fe, N. Mex.: Bear and Company, 1996.

Sarangerel. *Riding Windhorses: A Journey into the Heart of Mongolian Shamanism*. Rochester, Vt.: Destiny Books, 2000.

Schaefer, Stacy and Peter Furst, eds. *People of the Peyote: Huichol Indian History, Religion, and Survival*. Albuquerque, N. Mex.: University of New Mexico Press, 1996.

Somé, Malidoma Patrice. *Of Water and Spirit: Ritual, Magic, and Initiation in the Life of an African Shaman*. New York: Penguin Books, 1994.

Somé, Sobonfu. *Ritual: Power, Healing, and Community*. New York: Penguin Putnam Inc. 1993.

———. *The Spirit of Intimacy: Ancient African Teachings in the Ways of Relationship*. New York: William Morrow and Company, 1997.

Tacey, David. *The Edge of the Sacred: Transformation in Australia*. Blackburn, Victoria: HarperCollins, 1995.

Villoldo, Alberto and Erik Jendresen. *Dance of the Four Winds: Secrets of the Inca Medicine Wheel*. Rochester, Vt.: Destiny Books, 1990.

———. *Island of the Sun: Mastering the Inca Medicine Wheel*. Rochester, Vt.: Destiny Books, 1992.

Vitebsky, Piers. *The Shaman: Voyages of the Soul, Trance, Ecstasy, and Healing From Siberia to the Amazon*. New York: Little Brown and Company, 1995.

Whitaker, Kay Cordell. *The Reluctant Shaman: A Woman's First Encounter with the Unseen Spirits of the Earth*. New York: HarperCollins, 1991.

Whitley, David. *Following the Shaman's Path*. Ridgcrest, Calif.: Maturango Museum Press, 1998.

Wildish, Paul. *Principles of Taoism*. London: HarperCollins, 2000.

Wong, Eva, translator. *Seven Taoist Masters: A Folk Novel of China*. Boston: Shambala, 1990.

Zink, Nelson. *The Structure of Delight*. Santa Fe, N. Mex.: Mind Matters, 1991.

Business, Science, and Related

Albion, Mark. *Making a Life, Making a Living: Reclaiming Your Purpose and Passion in Business and in Life*. New York: Warner Books, 2000.

Bennis, Warren. *On Becoming a Leader*. Cambridge, Mass.: Perseus Books, 1989.

Block, Peter. *Flawless Consulting*. San Francisco: Jossey Bass Pfeiffer, 2000.

Bridges, William. *The Character of Organizations*. Palo Alto, Calif.: Davies-Black Publishing, 1992.

———. *The Human Side of Organizational Change*. Mill Valley, Calif.: William Bridges and Associates, 1993.

Fournies, Ferdinand F. *Coaching for Improved Work Performance*. New York: McGraw-Hill, 2000.

Freemantle, David. *The A-Z of Managing People*. Holbrook, Mass.: Adams Media Corporation, 1999.

Gilley, Jerry W. and Nathaniel W. Boughton. *Stop Managing, Start Coaching: How Performance Coaching Can Enhance Commitment and Improve Productivity*. New York: McGraw-Hill, 1996.

Greene, Robert. *The 48 Laws of Power*. New York: Penguin Putnam, 1998.

Guillory, William A. *The Living Organization—Spirituality in the Workplace*. Salt Lake City, Utah: Innovations International. 1997.

Hampden-Turner, Charles and Fons Trompenoors. *Mastering the Infinite Game: How Asian Values Are Transforming Business Practices*. Oxford: Capstone Publishing, 1997.

Jaworski, Joseph. *Synchronicity: The Inner Path of Leadership*. San Francisco: Berrett-Koehler Publishers, 1996.

Korten, David, C. *The Post-Corporate World: Life After Capitalism*. West Hartford, Conn.: Berrett-Koehler Publishers, 1999.

Mackay, Harvey. *Pushing The Envelope: All the Way to the Top*. New York: Ballantine Books, 2000.

Mathews, Christopher. *Hardball: How Politics Is Played Told by One Who Knows The Game*. New York: Harper and Row, 1988.

Pascale, Richard, Mark Millemann, and Linda Gioja. *Surfing the Edge of Chaos: The Laws of Nature and the New Laws of Business*. New York: Crown Business, 2000.

Ries, Al and Jack Trout. *The 22 Immutable Laws of Marketing*. New York: HarperBusiness, 1993.

Smith, Charles. *The Merlin Factor: Keys to the Corporate Kingdom*. Burlington, Vt.: Ashgate Publishing, 1997.

Stone, Douglas. Bruce Patton, and Sheila Heen. *Difficult Conversations: How to Discuss What Matters Most*. New York: Penguin Books, 1999.

Waldrop, M. Mitchell. *Complexity: The Emerging Science at the Edge of Order and Chaos*. New York: Simon and Schuster, 1992.

Wilson, Larry. *Changing The Game: The New Way to Sell*. New York: Simon and Schuster, 1987.

Zander, Rosamund Stone and Benjamin Zander. *The Art of Possibility: Transforming Professional and Personal Life*. Boston: Harvard Business School Press, 2000.

Index

A

absolute power, giving, 266
accepting whatever is, 15
achievement of power, 15; cost of announcing it too soon, 71–72; indifference to, 69–70 (*see also* detachment); options for, 29–31. *See also* failures; successes
acknowledgment, 42; of one's power, 51–53; of the potential of one's power, 6
acting without hesitation, 70–71, 241, 265
Adam and Eve, 77
allies, 150
"analysis paralysis," 182
anxiety: trap of, 156–57. *See also* fear; relaxation
arrogance, 243
artists, 104–6
assumptions, making no, 252–53
attachments. *See* detachment
attacking with lightning speed, 265–66. *See also* acting without hesitation
attending to implications, 235–36
attention, 42, 56, 218–19; focusing it in the present, 14–15. *See also* focusing
attentions, first and second, 124, 161; applied to business, 131–32; power and the second, 130–32, 135; primacy of the first, 125; qualities of the second, 126–30
"automatic," going on, 157–58
awareness of spirit, 31, 121

B

background of objects, focusing on, 133
balance, 15, 115–17, 123, 135; *vs.* imbalance, 78, 117–18
balancer, third communication style as, 183–85
balancing doing and being, 119–20
bidding for power. *See* power bids
bigger is not necessarily better, 28
breath, 168–69
business(es): the compelling game of, 22–24; looking to see where their real power lies, 29; questions for, 66–71; and the two attentions, 126, 131–32. *See also* stalking; work

C

Castaneda, Carlos, 178
challenges, xiii; backing away from excessive, 56–57; delaying facing, 57. *See also* skill level; test(s) of power; timing
cheating, 77–78, 96, 97
chiefs, 109–10
colors, matching, 236
commitment, 85, 260–61
communication, 16, 171, 191; basis of, 167–70; and the power of words, 167, 171–74; signs of invisible power in, 140–41
communication styles, 177–85; communicating between styles, 180; sequence of, 180–81
conception, 13, 43–44, 193–94
connecting: and becoming powerful, 208–10; *vs.* identifying, 211
connection, 190; disconnection and powerlessness, 208; inner, 211–13; restoring it in the village, 213–14
creativity, 105

D

death, 41
dependency, trap of, 156
detachment, 148; loss of, 157; state of, 41, 69–70, 254–55 (*see also* achievement

279

About the Authors

José and Lena Stevens have completed a ten-year apprenticeship with a high-degree Huichol shaman living in the Sierras of Mexico and have specific training with shamans in the Amazon and Andes regions of Peru. In addition, they have studied with and visited shamans in central Australia, Nepal, Finland, and the American Southwest. Lena has a background in business management and the arts. José received his master's degree from UC Berkeley and his doctorate in psychology from the School of Integral Studies in San Francisco.

Power Path Seminars™, José and Lena's coaching and consulting business, uses the principles outlined in their books. With Power Path Seminars, they bring their twenty-five years of experience to the business world through effective executive guidance programs, business retreats, trainings, and seminars. In addition, PPS provides accreditation and certification for consultants and coaches.

José and Lena are the authors of *Secrets of Shamanism: Tapping the Spirit Power within You* (Avon, 1988). In addition to many other books and articles, Dr. José Stevens is the author of *Transforming Your Dragons: Turning Fear Patterns into Personal Power,* released in 1994 by Bear and Company.

Together Dr. José Stevens and Lena Stevens have their base of operations in Santa Fe, New Mexico, and lecture internationally, teaching about principles of power, prosperity, personality types, communication styles, peak performance, and self-development. José has consulted with various individuals and businesses in Japan, Canada, Venezuela, Iceland, England, and Finland, and both Lena and José have led many tour groups to the ancient sacred sites of Egypt, England, the Yucatan, and Peru.

In addition, José and Lena provide consultation with lawyers, business leaders, scientists, and entrepreneurs from coast to coast and include Hollywood producers, actors, and screenwriters among their high-profile clients. They use their knowledge of shamanism and business psychology to privately coach and assist leaders to make difficult life decisions and to develop business strategy. Their diverse client group regularly reports powerful results.

Available products and services
through Power Path Seminars

- Quarterly newsletter offering cultural trends and current events articles
- Monthly tape subscription series forecasting the times and offering helpful hints
- Individual and group coaching and consultation
- Training seminars
- Certification programs
- Wilderness retreats, solos, and quests
- Continuing education

Check our Website for current schedule
of open classes, workshops, and other events:

Website: powerpathseminars.com
E-mail: pivotal@pivres.com
Power Path Seminars
P.O. Box 272
Santa Fe, New Mexico 87504-0272
Phone: (505) 982-8732

New World Library is dedicated to
publishing books and cassettes that inspire
and challenge us to improve the quality
of our lives and our world.
Our books and cassettes are available
at bookstores everywhere.
For a complete catalog, contact:

New World Library
14 Pamaron Way
Novato, California 94949

Phone: (415) 884-2100
Fax: (415) 884-2199
Or call toll free: (800) 972-6657
Catalog requests: Ext. 50
Ordering: Ext. 52

E-mail: escort@nwlib.com
www.newworldlibrary.com